Michael Van Valkenburgh Associates

RECONSTRUCTING URBAN LANDSCAPES

Yale University Press   New Haven and London

Michael Van Valkenburgh Associates

RECONSTRUCTING URBAN LANDSCAPES

Edited by Anita Berrizbeitia   Foreword by Paul Goldberger

Designed by Lorraine Ferguson.
Set in Nexus Sans and Nexus Serif
type by Lorraine Ferguson.
Printed in Singapore at Tien Wah
Press.

Library of Congress
Control Number: 2008939689

ISBN: 978-0-300-13585-5

A catalogue record for this book is
available from the British Library.

This paper meets the requirements
of ANSI/NISO Z39.48-1992 (Permanence
of Paper).

10 9 8 7 6 5 4 3 2 1

Jacket illustration:
Teardrop Park, New York.

pp. 2–3: **Marble tailings at the plaza
at the Boston Children's Museum.**

Contents

Paul Goldberger

Foreword

The connection between architecture and landscape architecture has never been simple, and it becomes almost maddeningly complex in the work of Michael Van Valkenburgh. Van Valkenburgh has an architect's sensibility, which is to say he thinks in terms of space and structure; he can feel the bones of a place. But he is at heart a plantsman, a lover of nature, and the realities and the demands of ecological systems shape his designs far more than any abstract patterns, shapes, or forms. To Van Valkenburgh, the relationship between the natural and the man-made is not a zero-sum game. He does not think that more design automatically means less nature, or that more nature has to mean less design. He wants to have the natural and the man-made, and he wants both in large measure. In a Van Valkenburgh park, you are as conscious of the built world as you are in the work of any architect. It is just that the built world that Van Valkenburgh presents you with is one in which design and nature engage in a subtle and often ambiguous dialogue, pushing, teasing, challenging the other in a way that makes you see everything, city and nature alike, with a striking intensity.

Van Valkenburgh is not one of those modernist landscape architects who you suspect would rather be designing buildings. He shows no interest in embracing the minimalist aesthetic of his architect colleagues, like so many of his fellow landscape designers. His work places no premium on austerity. It is not designed to create a seamless flow between building and open space, as if to show that the aesthetic of a piece of architecture could be extended right into a crafted landscape. You couldn't imagine Van Valkenburgh designing a plaza solely to set off a modernist building. At the very least he would engage the building, confront it, do all he could to remind us that nature is not the same as architecture—and that the point of landscape architecture is to make neither pure landscape nor pure architecture, but something else altogether.

Van Valkenburgh is no more interested in creating the pure image of *rus in urbe* than he is in distilling nature down to a set of abstract forms. There is no desire in his work to make the city disappear, no wish to have the natural landscape obscure the man-made one. He has referred to his work as "something more akin to the 'technological sublime' than a *rus in urbe*." By this measure Van Valkenburgh's work departs notably from that of Frederick Law Olmsted, whose massive shadow extends over all landscape architecture. For Olmsted, an urban park was a way of providing escape from the city, not connection to it. His Central Park may have been a completely manufactured landscape, but Olmsted did little to emphasize that and much to underplay it, as if he were quite willing to let you think that the park's designer was not Olmsted but God.

Van Valkenburgh makes no such suggestion, and I suspect that this is less a matter of ego than of realism. He wants to create a viable language of landscape design for the twenty-first century, and it is difficult, not to say futile, to build that language on the foundation of a rural illusion. His parks and public open spaces are based on the conviction that not only can the power of nature and the power of the man-made coexist, but they are the better for doing so.

Ultimately, of course, Olmsted believed the same thing; he just had a very different way of expressing it, a way shaped more by the Arcadian dreams of the nineteenth century than by the cosmopolitan preoccupations of the twentieth. If Olmsted saw nature as transcendental, Van Valkenburgh sees it as intensely emotional and stimulating, capable of invoking everything from serenity to the deepest social engagement. Nature to him is a force, a process, a set of things changing over time. In an Olmsted park, the picture is fixed, timeless and perfect. It changes only with the seasons. Olmsted parks are far more than just picturesque—they are intended always to be a backdrop to human activity—but the impulse toward the picturesque is ever present. To Van Valkenburgh, the scenographic is a form of historicism, and he wants none of it. He wants you to feel nature changing moment by moment, hour by hour, day by day, and to have you sense the layers of time. A sense of flux and movement means as much to him as visual image in creating the power of place.

Where Van Valkenburgh finds complete common ground with Olmsted is in his commitment to the notion of the public park as an expression of the democratic idea. Both landscape architects embrace the notion of public space as the equalizer, the place open to all where distinctions diminish, social classes fade into the background, and peaceful coexistence prevails. Van Valkenburgh shares Olmsted's democratic idealism. He has written of Olmsted's Prospect Park that "the pastoral Long Meadow is one of the greatest urban spaces in the country. Is anything more amazing than being there on a Sunday morning with thousands of people and their dogs?"

But Van Valkenburgh understands the difference between cherishing and protecting the great landscapes we have inherited, and imitating them. He is willing to learn from them—you sense that Olmsted will forever be a touchstone—but he is compelled to take it all in a new direction, toward a sensibility no less interested in beauty but shaped by the rough, uneven complexity of contemporary urban life. No Van Valkenburgh design begins with a clean slate. Every one of them starts with a series of givens: the natural history of a site, the built history of a site, the surrounding urban context. He seems never to wish these things away, however unpleasant they may appear to be—a history of industrial uses, some of them quite literally toxic, at Wellesley College; a series of mundane apartment towers looming over the relatively small site of Teardrop Park at Battery Park City in Lower Manhattan; a set of old factories, warehouses, and a noisy highway at Brooklyn Bridge Park, an industrial landscape that poses challenges that in some ways are more daunting than the vast, open riverfront that is this new 85-acre park's reason for being.

Van Valkenburgh's design for Brooklyn Bridge Park is the most ambitious large park conceived in New York since Robert Moses's designers expanded Riverside Park over the train tracks alongside the Hudson River on the Upper West Side in the 1930s. Riverside Park's Beaux-Arts formality, elegant by bureaucratic standards but more than a little stiff, was used mostly to divert attention from the fact that much of the park was, in effect, a flat roof over railroad tracks. The design tried, with varying degrees of success, to hide the West Side Highway as well, and it provided minimal access to the river, which was seen primarily as a source of visual splendor. With a site that in some ways is similar—a grand and compelling waterfront its great attraction, industrial elements its major challenge—Van Valkenburgh at Brooklyn Bridge Park reverses Moses's formula entirely. His interest is less in cushioning the interface between city and waterfront than in heightening their connection, in making the park a hinge that clamps the industrial city and the natural riverfront together, their joining creating a set of public spaces that will be both energizing and uplifting.

Van Valkenburgh has described the Brooklyn Bridge site as "a highly dynamic edge where two different but codependent ecosystems—river and city—merge. We have dwelled on revealing the water's edge in multiple ways, by changing its section, putting park visitors at water level, above it, and over it on causeways. This idea has less to do with a perfect moment (a landscape scene or picture) and more to do with creating in this park a series of unfolding spaces and sensory realizations. . . . basically, the Brooklyn Bridge Park project is about restoring complexity to the urban/river edge that was lost when the piers were built."

"Restoring complexity" in this case means a series of distinct landscapes, including gardens, playing fields, walkways and esplanades, and wetlands. They are arranged not in the formal order of either a Beaux-Arts or a minimalist landscape plan, but in response to the urban conditions on one side, and the riverfront on the other. Thus the park will have playgrounds at three entrance points to induce visitors to come in, a strongly defined entrance at the south end that Van Valkenburgh calls "an urban junction to compensate for Atlantic Avenue being ignored by the Brooklyn Queens Expressway design," and playing fields set in the middle, as a way of pulling people into the heart of the park. There will be a man-made marsh on a pier, reusing an industrial remnant in a manner not all that different from where its natural evolution might have taken it, and a variety of different edge treatments, from constructed boardwalks and floating edges to naturalistic rock edges. Van Valkenburgh has laid out the pathways to emphasize views to the greatest industrial artifacts the park has, the Brooklyn Bridge and the Manhattan Bridge, but you will often see them in surprising ways.

At Teardrop Park, a 1.75-acre park in lower Manhattan, the challenge could not have been more different: since the park's perimeter is tightly defined by new apartment buildings, it is more like an enormous outdoor room than anything else, entirely different from Brooklyn Bridge Park and also, more to the point, from its close neighbor, Battery Park City's long, landscaped waterfront promenade along the Hudson. Van Valkenburgh took that difference, in a sense, as his starting point, since the openness of the promenade made it reasonable to do what otherwise would have made no sense in a tight urban site, which is to make the park as dense as possible. It is counterintuitive, but it works, like the small room that feels bigger, not smaller, when it is filled with furniture. Van Valkenburgh divided the site in half—another counterintuitive move for a small park—with what he called the Notch, a cliff-like structure of bluestone. To the north went lawns, gardens, and a marsh, located so that they would be least often in shadow from the very tall building at the southern end of the site. To the south went more assertive topography in the form of high rock structures, play areas, a fountain, and a long slide. It is all, as Van Valkenburgh has said, a place of "intense robustness," responding to the tightness and banality of the apartment façades around it with variety and activity, filling up the space rather than letting it be.

Not the least of Van Valkenburgh's skills is the willingness to design densely in some situations and loosely and quietly in others, and, perhaps most important, the ability to know which should be which—which landscapes should be responded to with assertiveness, and which ones with deference. His work emerges out of a deep love of nature and a respect for its power and beauty, but also from an equal degree of love of the city, for its harshness and grit, and for the social gifts that urban life confers. He knows both the private joys of nature contemplated and the public joys of the city experienced, and he seeks not just to celebrate them but to enhance them both.

Anita Berrizbeitia

MVVA in Context

This anthology on the landscape architecture of Michael Van Valkenburgh Associates (MVVA) marks the twenty-seventh anniversary of the firm's founding. Established by Van Valkenburgh, the Charles Eliot Professor in Practice of Landscape Architecture at the Harvard University Graduate School of Design, the firm has grown from a handful of designers working on small, mostly private sites to an internationally known collaborative practice of more than fifty designers led by Van Valkenburgh, Matthew Urbanski, and Laura Solano, designing a diverse range of projects from gardens to complex urban landscapes.

This volume explores landscape architectural projects for urban sites that require complete or extensive reconstruction—a prevalent condition of lands available for development in post-industrial cities in North America and Europe. The preponderance of these types of projects in the firm's recent work has motivated shifts in their design approach and aesthetic sensibilities. Here, we analyze twelve projects that demonstrate these new directions of work.

MVVA was established at a time of critical transition in landscape architecture, characterized by the emergence of new approaches to the conceptualization and theorization of landscape. First, and most influential in the formation of a new sensibility for the emerging practices of the time, was the work of American earthwork artists such as Robert Smithson, Michael Heizer, Richard Long, Nancy Holt, and Mary Miss. In taking on the subject of landscape and the perception of phenomena in their work, these artists provided a powerful model against the reductive and functional design language of postwar modernism in American landscape architecture.[1] In 1979, art historian Rosalind Krauss demonstrated in her canonical essay "Sculpture in the Expanded Field" a method of analyzing earthworks that directly implicated the design fields (with her inclusion of the terms architecture and constructed site in the discussion), signaling a porosity that was to become increasingly prevalent between the fields of conceptual art and landscape architecture.[2]

Second, structuralism and the notion of type reopened the question of meaning and language in design, revealing the potential of historical precedent as a basis of formal invention. Both the work of the earthwork artists (reflecting a sensibility that favored the ephemeral and the projective over the fixed and the permanent) and the methodologies of structuralism

(as method to break from the rigid pairings of function with form, of program with type) allowed landscape architects to develop a self-consciousness about their own medium that had not been seen since the formal experiments of the avant-garde in the early decades of the century.[3] For although much had been accomplished by the previous generation—new concepts of space, new methods of applying ecology to design, and an expanded range of projects (from gardens and subdivisions to regional-scale projects) that built new working relationships with the urban design and planning fields—the profession had, by the early 1970s, yielded to a deadening pragmatism that left aside the poetics of the medium and largely rejected the value of landscape architecture's own languages and traditions. And although there had been other critiques against the overly reductive work of postwar modernism, such as the ecological movement of the 1960s and the social critiques of the 1970s, these had not produced alternative spatial configurations in answer to the questions of perception, expression, and form. The preference for the ephemeral and the open-ended, and the interest in language, were in turn supported by the dissemination of theories of interpretation and experience, hermeneutics and phenomenology, that along with structuralism became the core of design criticism and theorization. Equally important to substantiate the relationship between medium and meaning during this time was the arrival of cultural geography, itself reemerging as a reinvigorated field of study that drew on diverse theoretical traditions to explore the relationship between landscape and social, political, and cultural meanings.

Third, a renewed interest in the discipline's own language was accompanied by a renewed interest in gardens and their history. The venues for the dissemination of this information were numerous and varied. Exhibitions, publications, and journals, several of which were founded during the 1980s, uncovered landscapes and gardens as cultural practices in their own right.[4] Fourth, many public parks were built in Europe during the 1980s, as several metropolitan areas, most notably Paris, Barcelona, and London, began to transition, turning previous industrial sites, underutilized urban voids, and ports into public parks. One cannot underestimate the influence that this work had, and continues to have, on emerging American firms. The work built in Europe during this decade was innovative, formally strong, and contextual, addressing issues of history, site ecology, language, and program in synthetic ways. The abundance of design competitions during

Brooklyn Bridge Park site looking toward Manhattan. The most vital opportunities for waterfront park making today often are not planned on the expanding edge of urbanization (as in the nineteenth century), nor do they entail extensive land filling (as in the twentieth). Rather they involve redeveloping post-industrial sites within the city, sometimes at its very core.

this time also energized the field. Especially influential was the 1984 competition for the Parc de la Villette in Paris. Bernard Tschumi's winning entry, and OMA/Rem Koolhaas's proposal, presented radical and innovative approaches that generated a great deal of self-reflection among designers. Finally, environmentalism and ecology shifted from a specialized field of work within landscape architecture—primarily applied to large-scale regional sites—to a central concern for designers of all types of projects, including gardens and small urban parks.[5] These aesthetic and intellectual currents provided a rich and varied context out of which would spring MVVA's practice.

The first decade of MVVA was explored in the 1994 monograph *Design with the Land: Landscape Architecture of Michael Van Valkenburgh.*[6] By then, MVVA had consolidated its position as a critical practice that had absorbed the lessons of modernism while expanding the range of expressive and material possibilities of the landscape medium. The concerns with language, history, typology, and ecology that were at the center of disciplinary debates during the 1980s permeate the built works and projects presented in the monograph. The essays elaborate on the sensibilities for which MVVA became known: an interest in the expression of phenomena, time, and materiality; a deep and complex understanding of regionalism and context; and a new focus on the medium of landscape itself as content of the work. Of the seventeen projects featured in *Design with the Land*, twelve were small sites, of up to 20 acres (seven residential sites, five institutional or corporate sites), two were competitions, two were in-process master plans (for the Harvard Yard landscape in Cambridge, Massachusetts, and for the Ho-Am Art Museum and Sculpture Garden in Seoul, Korea), and MVVA's first public commission, the recently completed Mill Race Park in Columbus, Indiana. The sites for these projects were primarily on suburban lands, with clients who were patrons and collaborators, often from the art world, who supported Van Valkenburgh's early experimental work with garden design and installations. Since then, the focus of landscape architectural practice in the United States has changed significantly, as has Van Valkenburgh's practice.

During the last two decades, major American cities have been in transition from industrial to service economies. Many manufacturing, trade, transportation, and waste-disposal facilities built along waterfronts or at the edges of cities have been relocated, leaving behind urban land in need of remediation and reconstruction. In addition, cities have expanded around these marginal sites, incorporating them, so that former peripheral sites are now well within the boundaries of metropolitan areas. Thus in contrast to the suburban "green" sites of MVVA's first decade, of the twelve projects discussed here, six are in post-industrial sites, three are in sites prone to severe flooding, six are on platforms of inorganic land, and one has a disproportionately large quantity of impervious surfaces—roofs plus parking —that requires the design of an extensive stormwater management program. These contaminated, left-over, isolated sites bring unprecedented challenges that require new approaches to design. In contrast to the project sites of the early years, where design was hinged on relatively straightforward under-

The Teardrop Park site along the Hudson River was formed with landfill from foundation excavation of the World Trade Center in the 1960s.

standing of the ecological context (hardiness zone, soils, topography, climate, orientation, circulation, and relationship to architecture and program) and of the site's material, visual, and spatial character, the post-industrial sites of contemporary practice require a highly orchestrated collaborative process in which all aspects of a project have been thoroughly analyzed by numerous consultants, community members, clients, and MVVA's design team. In this realm of increasing technical and regulatory complexity, landscape architects, previously subconsultants to urban designers and architects, have become the prime consultants responsible for coordinating and synthesizing information from multiple disciplines, such as local, regional, and restoration ecology, civil and structural engineering, remediation, sustainability, architecture, transportation, planning, archeology, and preservation.

Changes in ecological theory over the last two decades have also had a significant impact on the practice of landscape architecture. Of special importance is a paradigm shift that explains the performance of ecosystems as dynamic rather than tending toward equilibrium, and open to unpredictable external events that will affect their evolution over time.[7] These changes led to a reconceptualization of landscape that emphasized a systems understanding of its components over a formally based one. In addition, digital technologies have made it possible to model ecological change and predict the effects of ecosystem dynamics on landscapes, enabling new ways to predict and project the performance of designed ecologies. Digital technologies have also expanded landscape architecture's formal repertoire, enabling the creation of complex spatial structures—such as gradients and drifts—that more closely respond to ecological ideas. The preservation and protection of the cultural heritage of sites, whether agricultural, industrial, or pre-colonial, have required design strategies that incorporate extant structures, significant vegetation, and other site features, creatively and sensitively reprogramming these elements for future uses. The multiple restrictions and regulations associated with the restoration of post-industrial sites and their transformation into publicly accessible recreational spaces have shifted the locus of innovation, in many instances, from the formal to the procedural. Formal and experiential decisions are, as a result, delayed to the last phases of design and determined as much by new technologies, logistical constraints, and regulations as by visual and site criteria. The work presented in this volume is especially influenced by new technologies, by a site's multiple histories, and by a commitment to innovate in the face of increased regulation and the constraints embedded in public processes.

Technology

Although it is not generally acknowledged in the extensive literature on MVVA, technical research was fundamental to Michael Van Valkenburgh's early work, in experimental design projects such as the ice walls, begun in 1979, the vine displays at the Regis Gardens of the Cowles Conservatory at the Walker Art Center, 1986–88, and the Vera List Courtyard at the New School for Social Research in New York.[8] In the early work technology was often used in

the service of form, for example, to give shape to the arches at the Regis Gardens, to build the circular walls of the Krakow Ice Garden, or to create the banded configuration of the garden at the Avenue Montaigne Courtyard, built on top of an underground parking garage. In recent projects, however, formal expression originates in, and is driven by, the technical challenges posed by the sites.

Technology is used most comprehensively in the ground, to reclaim it from a previous industrial use that has left the soil toxic, or to construct it from scratch, when it sits on a platform over occupied space or water. Although extensive technical interventions on the ground are routine, a greater range of technologies is needed to reconstruct and sustain environmental systems on degraded urban land. On "green," non-industrial sites, the underlying site logics, its geology and general drainage patterns, determined the design. In spite of extensive transformations for drainage and grading for programmatic requirements or aesthetic effects, these sites remained connected to their larger ecological setting. This is not the case, however, with post-industrial sites. These sites have been stripped of all traces of their history as pieces of larger landscape systems. Reconstructing the ground entails nothing less than reconstructing the connections among hydrological, vegetational, and soil systems. This is especially difficult to accomplish because the conditions left by industrial operations are often nearly irreversible.

To achieve a newly functioning ground, MVVA conceptualizes it first through its performative capacities—what it needs to do for the landscape above it to grow, evolve, and be self-sustaining over the long term. Thus the ground is constructed as a living and productive ecological system that will support multiple functions. As the source of nutrients, water, and oxygen,

Technology in the service of formal experiments in the early work of MVVA.

Left The Radcliffe ice walls, 1988.

Right The Vera List Courtyard at the New School, in collaboration with Martin Puryear.

Opposite The Regis Gardens of the Cowles Conservatory at the Walker Art Center, designed in 1986 with Barbara Stauffacher Solomon.

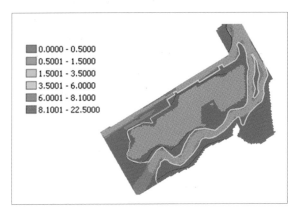

■	0.0000 - 0.5000
■	0.5001 - 1.5000
■	1.5001 - 3.5000
■	3.5001 - 6.0000
■	6.0001 - 8.1000
■	8.1001 - 22.5000

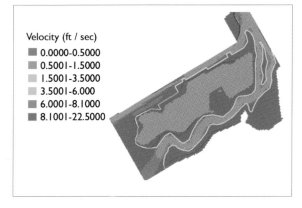

Velocity (ft / sec)

■	0.0000-0.5000
■	0.5001-1.5000
■	1.5001-3.5000
■	3.5001-6.000
■	6.0001-8.1000
■	8.1001-22.5000

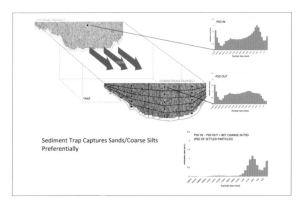

Sediment Trap Captures Sands/Coarse Silts
Preferentially

**Toronto Port Lands
Competition, 2007.**

Above Cross-section through
the proposed sediment basin.

Center, left and right Diagrams
showing the speed of
floodwater traveling through
the site.

Below Diagram showing
expected performance
of the Don River's proposed
sediment trap.

soil will support the establishment and future development of vegetation systems on the site. As surface it will conduct water, slowing it down to prevent erosion, holding it in place, temporarily or permanently as needed. Vertically, through its thickness, it will percolate water, recharging underground streams and aquifers. As it delivers water through to its depths, it will also cleanse it. As a porous skin, it will respond to external systems and changes in larger hydrological and climatic patterns, evolving in its own composition. The living organisms in the soil, such as microbes and worms, will exchange nutrients and chemicals with vegetation and other organisms, in a symbiotic relationship. In its load-bearing capacities, the ground will need to support weight without changing its surface's contours, and it will have to resist compaction from human use, so that it can continue to convey water and oxygen to roots and organisms that live between its particles. All of these invisible biological and ecological functions are as important as those we are able to see, such as durability, stability, comfort, and aesthetics.

Although in a sense one might expect that post-industrial sites are a tabula rasa that would afford a designer complete freedom of expression (because industrial operations have erased site conditions and severed connections to surrounding hydrological and topographical systems), they are not, and each project demands specific reconstruction techniques that, in turn, result in different ground conditions upon which a future landscape will develop. Thus, for example, the reconstruction of the ground at Alumnae Valley at Wellesley College entailed the construction of many layers with varied structural and biological properties, each with a different function. Some layers permanently encapsulate toxic soils, others contain surface flow, others release water slowly into the ground, while other layers perform their more typical functions as planting matrix. At the Toronto Port Lands, the ground is literally built from harvesting the sediment deposited by the Don River in a huge sedimentation basin at its mouth. This sediment is then cleansed through phytoremediation on the site, producing an initial landscape of furrows planted with sunflowers and other toxin-digesting plants. Remediation of the ground is conceptualized as a visible material determinant of the project, giving the landscape its primary character during the initial phases of the transformation of the industrial site into a public landscape.[9] Over time, the cleansed soil will be redistributed on the site to form the new bed of an estuary, a gradient ground condition from water to upland park. At Teardrop Park, a tiny 1.75-acre site on landfill in lower Manhattan, nine soil profiles, each with three horizons, were manufactured and assembled on the site to provide different conditions for varied planting regimens, for wetland, upland forest, and lawn. The ground here is understood as a matrix with built-in differentiation that will promote the establishment of ecological complexity on the surface. In addition, the ground beneath the lawn is reinforced with geofibers and geogrids, performing the job of stabilization that underlying geology, absent here, normally does, making the soil strong enough to keep a steeper than normal cross-sectional profile. At Brooklyn Bridge Park the ground is sculpted precisely to diminish the sound waves from the adjacent

Toronto Port Lands Competition. Proposed soil remediation process.

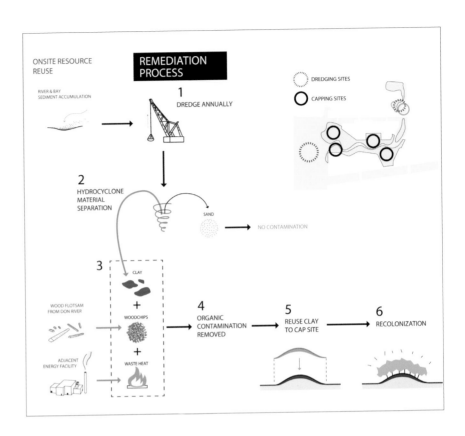

ONSITE RESOURCE
REUSE

REMEDIATION PROCESS

RIVER & BAY
SEDIMENT ACCUMULATION

○ DREDGING SITES

● CAPPING SITES

1 DREDGE ANNUALLY

2 HYDROCYCLONE MATERIAL SEPARATION

SAND

NO CONTAMINATION

3 CLAY

WOOD FLOTSAM FROM DON RIVER

+ WOODCHIPS

ADJACENT ENERGY FACILITY

+ WASTE HEAT

4 ORGANIC CONTAMINATION REMOVED

5 REUSE CLAY TO CAP SITE

6 RECOLONIZATION

Brooklyn Queens Expressway, and at Herman Miller it is shaped to reduce the speed of surface water, making it percolate through a constructed wetland, thus eliminating the conventional use of, and costs associated with, underground pipes to convey water.

Technology is used not only to reconstruct the ground but to assist nature to complete a cycle that has been severed permanently by previous industrial or urban use. At Wellesley, a pump will convey water up from the lake to the perched marsh in times of drought, and at Teardrop South three 8-foot-diameter heliostats track the movement of the sun and reflect its light into the park, which receives only four hours of sun per day. Also at Teardrop, underground water tanks cleanse gray water from adjacent buildings before reusing it for park irrigation. In many if not all of the projects presented in this volume, technology and nature have a kinship, an alliance that presents them as equal partners in a common goal of reconstruction.

Beyond the performative, technology is used as a means to intensify experience, to make processes and materials more powerfully visible. At Mill Race Park in Columbus, Indiana, the gravel quarry remnants are reshaped as positive figures against which the floods of the Flatrock and Driftwood rivers are measured. At the Allegheny Riverfront Park, the cantilevered platform at the water's edge was reconceptualized as a crust, a rough, hardened skin made of boulders that would trap pockets of soil, deposited by floodwaters, for vegetation. Here, and in MVVA's work generally, technique and materiality—the use of materials and their physical qualities as content of the

Teardrop Park.

Top Sun exposure diagram,
by Carpenter Norris Consulting,
commissioned by MVVA
to assess hours of available
sunlight and the sustainability
of turf grass.

Below Soils construction
documents. Nine soil profiles,
each with three horizons, were
designed and manufactured
to provide a wide range of
conditions for a diverse planting
palette to match the similarly
diverse microclimates. Biosolids
(composted sewage sludge)
and leaf compost were used
as organic amendments for
some of the soils.

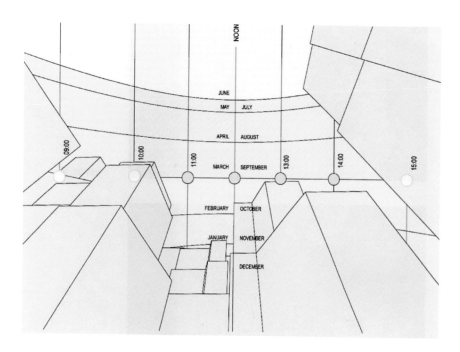

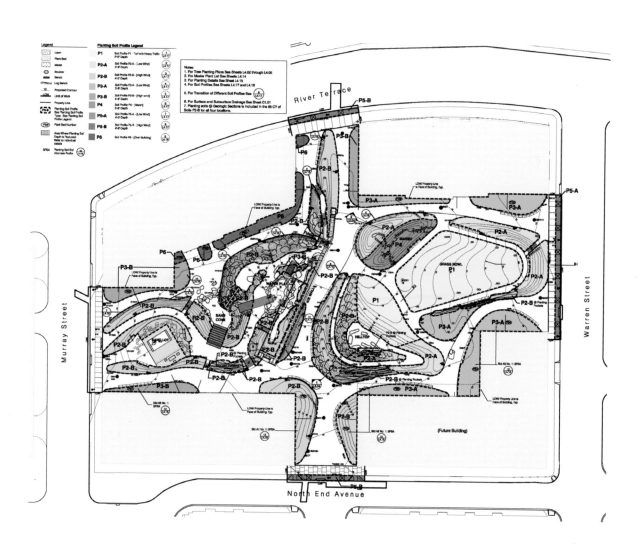

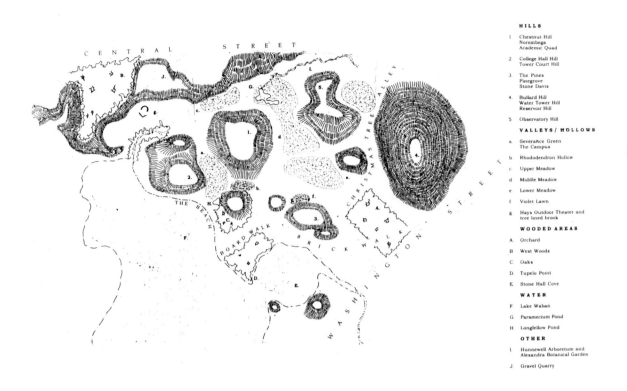

work—are in close alliance. Unlike conventional corporate practices, which tend to use a consistent set and combination of materials as a "signature" of their work, MVVA utilizes a broad spectrum of materials, chosen for each project as a response to site, region, program, and technology. Compare and contrast, for instance, the material intensity of the ground of the Tahari Courtyards, the toughness of the stone at Teardrop Park, the soft, fuzzy surfaces at Herman Miller, the already mentioned encrusted ground at Allegheny, and the delicacy of the grove at the Vera List Courtyard.

History

Landscapes that require extensive or total reconstruction raise the question of their relationship to the site's history. Reconstruction in this volume most often refers to the series of operations that will restore the site to a working ecosystem. Reconstructing urban landscapes does not mean, however, the restoration of those landscapes to a previous state. Such an ambition would be at the very least conceptually problematic (to which historical past—pre-industrial, colonial, pre-colonial—does one restore, and why?) and most likely unsustainable in the long run.

    The notion that landscapes build upon previously existing landscapes, without completely erasing the marks left behind by earlier uses, informs much of the work included here. At Mill Race Park, artifacts found on the

Wellesley College.
Elizabeth K. Meyer's diagram of landform structure and landscape types.

Opposite **Herman Miller Factory.** Aerial view of the east meadow.

site—such as the covered bridges, the gravel pits, and the allée of lindens—became the starting point of the design. At Brooklyn Bridge Park, the adaptive reuse of the old port facilities, the piers and warehouses, establishes a material and spatial continuum at the waterfront that is inclusive of the varied histories of the site. Similarly, in the competition entry for the High Line, the remnant rail line in New York's West Side, the conservation of extant ecologies that had colonized the abandoned structure for more than three decades became the central object and subject of MVVA's proposal.

Several of the projects examined here have required remediation techniques mandated by state environmental laws that preclude reconstruction to a significant historical period or self-sufficient ecological system. At Alumnae Valley at Wellesley College, levels of toxicity on the ground and radical changes in topographical and drainage patterns required that an ecological restoration prevail over a historical one. Further, these two agendas were not always entirely compatible, and MVVA faced a balancing act in which remediation, restoration of the hydrological function of the valley, ecology, and the present needs of the college had to be reconciled with Olmsted's 1921 vision for the campus. The reconstruction of the mouth of the Don River, where it meets the shores of Lake Ontario in Toronto, Canada, has likewise required a great deal of ecological reconstruction without the possibility of restoring the river to a pre-industrial condition. In their winning competition proposal for the Toronto Port Lands, titled "Port Lands Estuary," river dynamics provide the main criteria for urban design on the defunct port facilities of Toronto, yet what was restored was the performance of the river, not its form or location, from its current bound and controlled, channelized condition to a dynamic hydrological system open to fluctuations of water volume, with associated shifts in vegetation and wildlife populations.

Ecological and remediation techniques for reconstruction are the primary, but not the only, criteria for reconstruction. Canonical works of landscape architecture remain an important source of reference for MVVA, although the information drawn from historical landscapes, designers, and artists is not always formal or stylistic. For example, the Olmsteds' legacy surfaces in different ways across the firm's recent projects. For the reconstruction of Alumnae Valley, MVVA learned overall site logistics and structure from Frederick Law Olmsted, Jr.'s 1921 plan for the campus, but did not draw from Olmstedian aesthetics to develop the visual character of the valley landscape. Paradoxically, because it is a small site compared to Wellesley and to the typical Olmstedian landscape, at Teardrop Park the visual references to Olmsted are more direct, although still not literal. Here MVVA wanted to achieve what Olmsted called "psychological range," a term that MVVA interprets as breadth of experience afforded by, in the case of this tiny site, the intricacy and variety of material conditions, the references to experiences of landscapes elsewhere, and the sense of compression followed by release as one passes through the arch and climbs to the top of the lawn—all of which are experiences that one finds in New York's Central Park, albeit achieved via

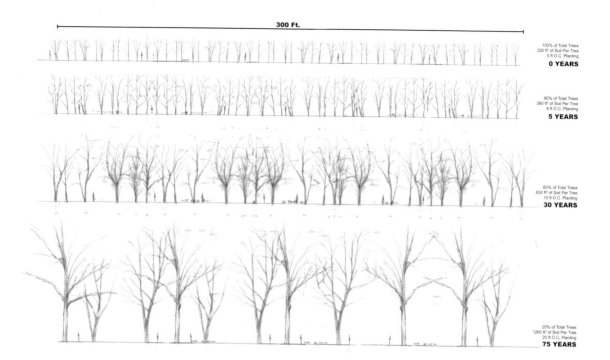

100% of Total Trees
330 ft³ of Soil Per Tree
5 ft O.C. Planting
0 YEARS

90% of Total Trees
380 ft³ of Soil Per Tree
6 ft O.C. Planting
5 YEARS

60% of Total Trees
630 ft³ of Soil Per Tree
10 ft O.C. Planting
30 YEARS

20% of Total Trees
1260 ft³ of Soil Per Tree
20 ft O.C. Planting
75 YEARS

different means. Finally, Olmsted's technique of cutting away soil to expose bedrock and make geology a palpable presence on the landscape, a procedure used extensively in Central Park, informed the grading of the east meadows at the Herman Miller factory landscape. The history of form and techniques, the natural and geological histories, land use history, social history, and the history of materials management on the site are brought together in the process of reconstruction to understand how and why the site got to its present state, and how to guide it toward a future. All of these are given equal value at one point or another, as different types of history are recalled to inform different aspects of a project.

Innovation

Plants are a primary element and key to design at MVVA, and innovation with planting design began early in the firm's history. Van Valkenburgh was deeply influenced by the rural landscapes of his childhood in upstate New York, developing sensibilities there that were further refined at Cornell's College of Agriculture and at the University of Illinois (Urbana-Champaign), where he trained in landscape architecture. When MVVA was founded, in 1982, Van Valkenburgh also began his teaching career at the Harvard University Graduate School of Design, where he was hired to teach the planting design courses. At Harvard, Van Valkenburgh encountered an intellectual climate, primarily within the architecture department, that was focused on debates around the uses of historical types in contemporary architecture. For Van Valkenburgh,

**Brooklyn Bridge Park.
Evolution and management
of proposed park hedgerows
as planned for a seventy-
five-year period.**

the ecological approach to plants was paradigmatic in providing a rationale for the way vegetation worked as living systems, but the formal and spatial implications of ecology were yet to be made. Indeed, by the late 1970s, planting design had fallen victim to polarizing debates between designers and ecologists: do you begin with an abstract spatial structure and then assign the best plant for that structure (the designers' approach), or do you begin with the most appropriate species for the site, and let the choice of plants inform the formal and spatial structure (the ecologists' approach)? In his new plants classes, Van Valkenburgh conflated an ecological approach with one that was typological and language driven. Although this may seem standard today, it represented a substantial conceptual leap then, one that bridged the nature vs. art schism to provide an alternative that was inclusive of both. The planting design classes that took place during the following years provided Van Valkenburgh with a setting for experimentation that generated many creative applications in his practice. Several of these can be seen in the early projects published in *Design with the Land*. Of particular importance is the maple thicket planted at the Vera List Courtyard. Here, for the first time, MVVA used liner stock, 1-inch-caliper saplings used by nurserymen to start a field, and usually not available for retail, as the starting point of the project. The lightness of the liner stock allows great flexibility in experimenting with the layout of the plants and in developing, over time, new spatial configurations. Sixty container-grown maple saplings were planted as close as 2 feet apart to create the sense of a grove in this small urban courtyard. As the trees have matured in their first decade of growth, MVVA staff (the New York office is only a few blocks away) thin them out annually, three or four at a time, allowing character to develop in unexpected ways while the plants adapt to their environment. This planting strategy is a significant departure from traditional planting techniques in which landscape architects specify the largest possible plants for the given budget. Clients are rarely willing to wait years before vegetation matures and the intended effects of the design begin to materialize. This sets the spatial structure for the project from the beginning and limits the landscape's basic condition of dynamic change. By working with much younger plant material, typically considered undesirable, MVVA created new planting strategies and spatial typologies, and shifted client sensibilities toward an appreciation for the ephemeral and dynamic qualities of the maples as they evolve from young thicket to mature grove. This technique would later be applied in other situations. At the Allegheny Riverfront Park, the 1,480 boulders that form the surface of the lower park did not leave much room for full-grown plants with large root balls. MVVA again used liner stock that, in addition to fitting within crevices, allowed them to specify greater numbers of trees, to re-create the same sense of raw vegetation that one finds upstream along the edge of the Allegheny River, and to increase the survival odds of the trees by letting them adapt to less than optimal conditions early in their life, in this tough flood-prone site.

Experimentation with planting typologies is ongoing at MVVA. At Harvard Yard, MVVA replaced the monoculture of American elms with thirty

Residential projects at MVVA often provide the opportunity to experiment with design language, techniques, and materials. In this stream bank stabilization project MVVA installed live stakes, a technique borrowed from restoration practices, to prevent soil erosion.

different species to avoid the risk of losing all of the trees in the event of disease. However, because the effects produced by the vase-shaped crown of elm trees were still desirable, over the last fifteen years the lower branches of the new trees have been incrementally removed to simulate the effect of the canopy of the elm. Eventually the specific form of each species will be sublimated in favor of a spatial structure that is uniform and transparent, thus preserving the effects of the original planting while providing for an ecologically diverse plant palette. Another innovation with planting design that conflates the ecological with the typological is, for example, the miniature forest at Teardrop Park, where the spacing of understory trees is carefully manipulated to give the illusion of upper-canopy forest. MVVA also adapts techniques from the horticulture, agriculture, forestry, and restoration industries for use in the design and construction of urban landscapes. For example, they contracted with a nursery to develop clump forms of trees by planting 2-inch-caliper single-trunk saplings with their rootballs touching. Live stakes—live, woody cuttings that are tamped into the soil to root, grow, and create a living root mat that stabilizes the ground by reinforcing and binding soil—is another example of how MVVA transfers technologies from the forestry and restoration industries into their projects.

In spite of their insistence on ecology as fundamental to practice, MVVA is not purist in its use of plants; it often combines native with non-native species to create specific effects. River birch (*Betula nigra*) with yellow groove bamboo (*Phyllostachys aureosulcata*), sweetbay magnolia (*Magnolia virginiana*) with bamboo, witch hazel (*Hamamelis virginiana*) with bamboo,

Teardrop Park.
Michael Van Valkenburgh and
Michael Mercil discussing
Ann Hamilton's *Geologic Section*
with Betsy Hoffman, who
oversaw the mason's work.

Japanese cryptomeria (*Cryptomeria japonica*) with dawn redwood (*Metasequoia glyptostroboides*), and plane trees (*Platanus x acerifolia*) with pin oak (*Quercus palustris*) are some of the unusual combinations of plants that have been installed in recent projects. Further, the use of ecology and process shifts from project to project, depending on the site, its larger processes, and the intended program. Ecology can be technique (Herman Miller), expression (Mill Race), or analogy (Tahari). More often, such as at Teardrop Park, MVVA uses ecological and horticultural practices within the same site, presenting a gradient of plant palettes that transitions from the native and naturalistic (in the wetland garden) to the exotic and formalistic (in the hellebore hill).

     In the work of MVVA, innovation occurs as much in the formal and visual layers of the project as it does in the manipulation of regulations that control the range of potential experiences on sites. The Americans with Disabilities Act (ADA) codes, environmental regulations, labor relations, and stringent budgets are turned into the stuff of creative manipulation, driving forces for innovation and transformation in design. For example, at Allegheny Riverfront Park, MVVA had to research and question every piece of regulation that related to the project to find opportunities to overcome the difficulty of the site, and it is here that the locus for innovation is identified. Not only was the site extremely challenging (with an average width of 31 feet and a length of 3,700 feet), squeezed between river and highway, but it had overlapping jurisdictional areas, each with different regulations. To create a context in which a park was even possible, MVVA intervened in areas traditionally outside the realm of landscape architecture—traffic engineering and urban roadway standards. MVVA found and applied the arguments that would relocate the roads in order to consolidate park space and make it less of a left-over space. Further, they redesigned the engineer's elements and standard details (like center lanes, turning radii, curb details, etc.) within the limits set by regulations, yet in such a way as to make the park and its landscape the visually dominant feature in this massive piece of urban infrastructure. After all the battles were fought, MVVA succeeded in the unthinkable: making decisions usually left to highway engineers who, in addition to professional leverage, had the federal funds to implement the project.

Another significant discovery in the research for the Allegheny Riverfront Park was the amount of latitude that exists within ADA codes for handrail design. Looking for creative avenues within the structure of the code led to the unique design of the ramp/handrail system, which allowed MVVA to create a visually dynamic railing profile independent of the sequence ramp/landing, thus achieving a rail that descends from the boulevard level all the way to the river with a continuous slope.

At Teardrop Park, the locus for innovation was labor regulations within New York City. These regulations prohibit landscape architects from making adjustments to the placement of stones in a wall once construction has begun. Artists, however, are allowed to compose and shift heavy stones in situ as many times as necessary to satisfy their aesthetic program. Indeed, artist Ann Hamilton composed and built her "geologic sections" at Teardrop Park in this manner. Wanting to build a wall of nonstandard natural stones, which cannot be fully described in construction documents that are subject to public bidding (because their size and shape cannot be preestablished and thus priced accurately), MVVA was forced to rethink the construction process. The wall was designed and built at the stone quarry, far outside New York City, then each piece was numbered and its location in the massive 60-foot-long wall recorded before it was carefully taken apart. Once transported to the site in downtown Manhattan, it was reassembled by union laborers, like pieces in a previously determined puzzle.

A similar strategic move occurred at Brooklyn Bridge Park, where MVVA wanted to allow park users direct engagement with the water, instead of providing the conventional experience of looking at the water from an elevated pier. Environmental regulations prohibit increasing, beyond what already exists on the site, the amount of shade cast over water. "Shade swapping"—removing the surface of an existing pier and taking the equivalent amount of square footage to build floating boardwalks, boat launches, and a safe-water area for kayakers—allowed MVVA to comply with environmental regulations and create a complex edge where recreation coexists with nature, bringing new experiences into the city. By intervening in things that are believed to be immutable or of no importance, MVVA makes the point that the tools of the designer are not just formal, organizational, technical, or material but lie as well in the strategic manipulation of regulatory practices.

Project Essays

The projects chosen for this volume are presented chronologically to offer a sense of how the firm's work has evolved as it responded to increasingly difficult conditions in marginal sites. Thus the essays begin with Mill Race Park in Columbus, Indiana, the first post-industrial commission of the firm, and end with the 2007 winning scheme "Port Lands Estuary," the largest ecological, remediation, and urban design proposal the firm has undertaken.

Most writing about contemporary landscape architecture focuses on situating the work within larger cultural ideas, tracing the connection between those ideas and their physical manifestations on the land. While this places greatest emphasis on the cultural project of landscape, and rightly so, it typically discusses projects in their completed state. For this volume, the authors were charged with situating their writing at the intersection of the conceptual and the practical, that is, on the negotiations that must be made between design intent, the realities, often unanticipated, of the site, and the challenges of questioning codes and regulations to transform them into a design language.

Jane Amidon examines Mill Race Park as a "cusp" landscape of seminal importance to MVVA's work, because it exhibits a strong interest in formalism, reminiscent of MVVA's earlier modernist work, alongside a new agenda to embrace and reveal the ephemeral, temporal, and formless phenomena of nature. At this former site of an industrial tannery, MVVA first faced questions of toxicity, cultural heritage, and reuse that they would confront many times thereafter.

In "Material, Event, Sensation," Amidon describes how MVVA coaxed a park out of a thin strip of land between a river and a major urban highway through the manipulation of highway engineering standards to gain a few feet here and there, the close reading of ADA regulations to discover room for flexibility, and the projection of a cantilevered walk over the river. Beyond these opportunistic strategies, the addition of intense material effects that amplify topographical, hydrological, and planting references makes the Allegheny Riverfront Park transcend the limitations imposed by its host infrastructure to offer recreational, visual, and phenomenological experiences that engage contemporary urban culture.

The limitation of the Herman Miller Factory site was not lack of space but the management of vast quantities of stormwater in a project with no budget for landscape. Taking over the job and the budget from civil engineers, MVVA devised a stormwater management system that was to take place entirely on the surface, as a series of wetlands intertwined with parking. The monumental earthworks, the entry allée, the expansive meadows, and the overscaled light masts result in a landscape that, although entirely functional, challenges the positivism of site engineering to provoke in the visitor an aesthetic response, one Elissa Rosenberg describes as akin to the sublime because of the powerful and minimalist scale of its elements.

Small gardens continue to be seminal for MVVA, even though the firm increasingly takes on more prestigious urban design projects, because they afford the opportunity to experiment and reposition the work. Linda Pollak describes how the material plenitude that saturates the tiny gardens in the Tahari Courtyards, coupled with spatial strategies that diminish the effects of the surrounding glass walls, creates an engrossing environment that radically alters this ancient garden type, as well as the daily experience of this office and warehouse complex in suburban New Jersey.

Peter Fergusson describes both the challenges and the compromises that had to be made when balancing remediation technologies, budgets, and the hydrological function of Wellesley's Alumnae Valley. The impossibility of restoring this landscape to a self-sustaining functional ecosystem raises questions about the role of ecology in post-industrial landscapes. Fergusson argues that ecology alone is insufficient, and that the incorporation of metaphor, mnemonic devices, and representation is fundamental in the conceptualization and reshaping of nature.

In "Elective Affinities," Erik de Jong argues that successful landscape architecture brings forth emotional responses, awakening an individual's inherent capacity to summon deeply felt affinities with the natural world. The remarkable feat here is that Teardrop Park, a very small site encased by four large apartment buildings, nevertheless elicits such a response. Through the use of sectional strategies, scalar manipulations, material intensity, and advanced technologies for ground stabilization, irrigation, and planting, the tiny size of the neighborhood park recedes in the face of the wealth of experiences contained within.

In her essay, "A Landscape-Based Approach to the Design of Three Plazas," Rachel Gleeson examines recent plaza projects. What distinguishes these projects from the historical type—the plaza as the void left over from the construction of the city—is that they do not derive their identity solely from the image of the surrounding architecture. MVVA hybridizes the type into a plaza/garden by inserting landscape—as visual phenomenon, as system, and as symbol—to reconstruct the identity of these spaces as pieces of their larger environments.

The contemporary urban landscape is as much the result of public processes and community involvement as it is of design. Ethan Carr's essay on the Brooklyn Bridge Park positions MVVA's design for the industrial water-front at the intersection of community activism and ecological thinking. Addressing many of the mandates of the adjacent neighborhoods, MVVA reconceptualized the waterfront through the ecological concept of a complex edge, a dynamic territory that is the result of the interaction between water, city, local politics, and social programs.

Finally, Andrew Blum speaks of the metaphorical content of the ecological reconstructions of MVVA, a new poetics of what he calls the Eco-City Beautiful that moves beyond ecology as illustrative or didactic. He describes MVVA's use of ecology in two recent proposals as a holistic approach that is equal parts measurable science and cultural content, ultimately defining a new form of civic virtue.

Teardrop Park.
Aerial view showing the site
bounded by tall apartment
buildings that cast long
shadows onto the space.

Conclusions

The work chosen for this volume demonstrates the growing complexity of
the practice of landscape architecture as it increasingly deals with sites
of uncertainty and contradiction, with unpredictable sources for financing,
environmental regulations, and public processes that may take decades to
come to fruition. Further, it shows that the result of the negotiations among
larger ecological systems, existing site conditions, and past and future programs is far from formulaic. Nevertheless, we can see several tendencies in
MVVA's work in the last decade and a half, as it responds to changes in the
conditions of practice. First, as is true of other leading practices today, MVVA
has a much expanded role in public projects during the early planning phases,
when frameworks for design begin to emerge and opportunities for new
interaction between parks and cities are open. In projects such as the Toronto
Port Lands and the Brooklyn Bridge Park, MVVA takes on the tasks of financial
planners, advocates, community mediators, and public relations professionals,
in addition to orchestrating design at many scales. Second, there is a shift
in the role of remediation technologies in the conceptualization and
reconstruction of landscapes. Whereas fifteen to twenty years ago soil and
water remediation was strictly a technical operation separate from the process
of landscape making, as it happened in Mill Race Park, today it is a generative
element in a project, a determinant of its forms. Generating a landscape
that evolves out of the technical program of reconstruction has become a
priority of the firm's work. Third, alongside remediation and reconstruction
processes comes the question of reestablishing connections to larger
surrounding ecological systems of a site. The current environmental crisis
tells us that nature must have priority in the decision-making process and,
indeed, MVVA prioritizes ecological reconstructions in their work. But
for MVVA nature's requisites alone are not sufficient to engage fully questions
of experience, of nature's representation, or of program. Further, unlike
earlier environmental practices where there was a consistent image of
nature—identical in every project, regardless of site—MVVA rejects the idea
that there is an accepted view of what nature in urban sites ought to be.
The work in this volume shows ecology and nature existing along a full
spectrum, from the purely pragmatic to the purely symbolic. Fourth, form, as
a precisely determined and stable component of the landscape, is as present
in MVVA's recent work as it was in the early years of the practice. However,
form emerges much later in the design process, and it is conditioned by many
criteria outside traditional landscape vocabularies. Still, site remains a critical
determinant of the projects presented here. Yet it is as much an inspiration
as it is a point of departure in the work of MVVA. Beyond satisfying all
environmental, economic, programmatic, and community criteria, MVVA
introduces an intense materiality—by foregrounding the physical, tactile,
temporal, and phenomenological aspects of landscape—to augment,
sometimes even distort, those unique qualities of a site that lead to memorable
experiences.

Finally, questions of meaning and content continue to be of fundamental importance in the work of MVVA, and this is especially so when it is impossible to achieve a full and sustainable reconstruction, such as at Wellesley, or when the sites are completely artificial, such as at Teardrop or Tahari. As several authors have discussed, translations—the making of spatial, material, or ecological choices that have visual implications—are required to take a project from an idealized model of nature to the realities of an urban or post-industrial site. Situated between a critical naturalism and a critical rationalism, MVVA strategically turns logistical, organizational, and infrastructural aspects of the landscape into a poetics of the medium, one that resides at the intersection of the firm's own spatial and material sensibilities, the conditions left by a site's previous histories, the projection of future ecologies and social programs, and the motivation to reassert the power of landscape in the cultural imagination.

Notes

1 Michael Van Valkenburgh, George Hargreaves, Martha Schwartz, Peter Walker, Kathryn Gustafson, Maya Lin, Hannsjörg Voth, and Dani Karavan, for example, were greatly influenced by this work.

2 Rosalind Krauss, "Sculpture in the Expanded Field," in *The Originality of the Avant-Garde and Other Modernist Myths* (Cambridge, Massachusetts: MIT Press, 1988): 276–290.

3 For details on the avant-garde of the second decade of the twentieth century, I refer the reader to Marc Treib's *Modern Landscape Architecture: A Critical Review* (Cambridge, Massachusetts: MIT Press, 1993): 68–88, and to Dorothée Imbert's *The Modernist Garden in France* (New Haven: Yale University Press, 1993), specifically the work of Gabriel Guevrekian and Robert Mallet-Stevens.

4 Michael Van Valkenburgh curated two important exhibitions during the 1980s. The first, *Built Landscapes: Gardens in the Northeast* (1983), an exhibition of twentieth-century works by five American landscape architects, showed at the Brattleboro Museum and Arts Center, Brattleboro, Vermont, Gund Hall Gallery, Harvard University Graduate School of Design, and Wave Hill, New York. The second, *Transforming the American Garden: Twelve New Landscape Designs* (1986), examined the garden as laboratory for experimentation in the work of contemporary landscape architects. Other notable exhibitions were the San Francisco Museum of Modern Art's *Lawrence Halprin: Changing Places* (1986), and *Peter Walker: Experiments in Gesture, Seriality, and Flatness* at the Harvard University Graduate School of Design (1989). In 1991, the Museum of Modern Art, New York, had a retrospective on Brazilian landscape architect Roberto Burle Marx titled *Roberto Burle Marx: The Unnatural Art of the Garden. The Journal of Garden History, Landscape Journal, Gartenkunst,* and *Pages Paysages,* for instance, all began during the 1980s.

5 See Elizabeth K. Meyer, "The Post-Earth Day Conundrum: Translating Environmental Values into Landscape Design," in *Environmentalism in Landscape Architecture,* Michel Conan, ed. (Washington, D.C.: Dumbarton Oaks, 2000): 187–244. Meyer discusses the work of emerging designers during the late 1970s and early 1980s such as Van Valkenburgh, George Hargreaves, and Susan Child, and the writings of Catherine Howett, as important early efforts to translate environmental values into aesthetic practices.

6 Edited by Brooke Hodge, with essays by James Corner, Paula Deitz, Peter Rowe, and John Beardsley (New York: Princeton Architectural Press, 1994).

7 H. Ronald Pulliam and Bart R. Johnson, "Ecology's New Paradigm: What Does It Offer Designers and Planners?" in *Ecology and Design,* Bart R. Johnson and Kristina Hill, eds. (Washington, D.C.: Island Press, 2002): 51–84.

8 At the Regis Gardens, experiments were conducted to determine the growth response of the creeping ficus vine to thirty-four variations of soil mixtures and different irrigation protocols. At the Vera List Courtyard, the small, 4,500-square-foot garden built over a slab and surrounded by tall buildings, MVVA mapped areas of extreme light conditions to break the stasis of the enclosed space and augment microclimatic differences through the choice of plants. The wheelchair ramp is built on pylons to provide space for the tree roots to extend back and forth, under the ramp, as much as possible.

9 Remediation technologies usually involve chemical processes through which soil and water are cleansed in situ of toxins deposited by previous industrial uses or by polluted surface run-off. Phytoremediation is a technology that uses the biological functions of plants, such as transpiration and chelation, to extract contaminants from water and soil.

Mill Race Park

Jane Amidon

Mill Race Park
At the Threshold

MILL RACE PARK
Columbus, Indiana
85 acres
Completed in 1993

Liminal: of or at the threshold, where one condition crosses over into another

Public parks are zones of material and social compression, where users confront edited versions of physiographic and societal circumstances. While acreage and location determine unique degrees of complexity in the branding, programming, implementation, and management of public grounds, common currents can be identified across a spectrum of scales and orientations that anchor a park's making to a specific generation. Significantly, it is the moment of typological transition, where aspects of the old persist while strategies of the new are introduced, that represents critical shifts in cultural perspective and technological capacities. Mill Race Park, at the flood-prone convergence of the Flatrock and Driftwood rivers on the outskirts of Columbus, Indiana, is just such a cusp landscape, occupying proto-postmodernist terrain between formalism and process dynamics.

Opened in 1993, Mill Race began a period of park making in the practice of MVVA that evolved alongside the profession's and the public's shifting attitudes about nature and urban parks in the late twentieth and early twenty-first centuries. As designed landscapes morphed from the form-intensive, late-modernist logic of field-and-figure toward the contextualization of site as amplified material process, public parks became increasingly literal in their response to physical environs. Although maintaining aspects of formalism, the new landscapes of this era were conceptually driven by the duality of event and recovery: daily tidal flux, growth and harvest, and seasonal phenomena were cycles to be embraced and revealed by design, not defended against. For Van Valkenburgh and his associates, the 85-acre Mill Race Park was the first opportunity to realize ideas, writ large, with which he and the profession had been experimenting for several years at the smaller garden scale.[1]

Both the conceptual and the geographic identities of Mill Race Park suggest liminal terrain. The park speaks simultaneously of genius loci—an authenticity of place revealed by the performance of regional matter—and of abstraction, via the introduction of idealized form. This is an apt stance for public grounds in the community of Columbus, a small midwestern city renowned for its deep roots in agriculture and industry, as well as for its impressive but somewhat alien collection of modernist and contemporary works of architecture, landscape architecture, urban infrastructure, and art.[2] Mill Race Park not only offered an emerging landscape architect his first

Crowds at the amphitheater spill onto the surrounding lawn and under the shade of large canopy trees.

45

50 Avenue Montaigne, the General Mills headquarters, and Mill Race Park, all designed during the early 1990s, mark the transition between formalism and process dynamics in the work of MVVA.

The garden at 50 Avenue Montaigne (Paris, France, 1993). Rows of clipped hornbeam and espaliered lindens established a structural clarity that defined spatial volume, provided an armature for art and water features, and highlighted seasonal change.

At the General Mills Headquarters Entry Garden (Minneapolis, Minnesota, 1991), an unmowed field of native prairie grasses scattered with loose groupings of river birch was burned annually to renew the meadow, a management technique specific to the region, used by Native American and early cattle ranchers to promote the health of the grassland. The garden was removed in the late 1990s.

Aerial view of Mill Race Park at flood stage.

major public commission (Van Valkenburgh left full-time teaching and established a staffed office upon receiving the Mill Race contract) but also was a chance for Columbus to open its first sizable park. Before the park could be realized, however, constraints produced by the site's location, history, and current use had to be addressed. Foremost among these were flooding and, to a lesser degree, contamination. Bracketing the technical issues was a philosophical challenge implicit in the park's seemingly incompatible constituencies. On one side was the local audience (park users), on the other, Van Valkenburgh's professional milieu—international colleagues and design critics who would be evaluating the park as much on its theoretical merits as on its utility. The project was commissioned by the Columbus Parks and Recreation Department, its design fees paid by the Cummins Engine Foundation. It would be constructed by neophyte Job Corps trainees on a minimal budget funded primarily by donations. To succeed it had to be affordable, resilient, relatively simple to build, and conceptually rigorous.

Site: Conditions and Constraints

Mill Race Park sits in an oxbow bend between the Flatrock River and the western edge of downtown Columbus, just above the confluence at which the Flatrock and the Driftwood meet to form the east branch of the White River.[3] Beginning in the late 1800s, the site was occupied periodically by a tannery, 26 acres of gravel pits, and worker housing. Nicknamed "Death Valley," the parcel at the outskirts of current-day business and residential precincts was isolated by rail tracks, but for decades had been used informally by locals for recreation. Infrastructural residue from past operations became orientation devices for the park scheme. Van Valkenburgh's embrace of "positive" contamination allowed the design to edit rather than fully supplant the site's cultural (his)stories. For example, across the central and upper portions of

The back side of the earthen amphitheater offers a more ambiguous and scale-less presence in the park.

the park, three historic bridges (one relocated from off site) were retained as links and focal points within pedestrian and vehicular circuits. Four-foot-high tannery wall remnants along the eastern boundary became a datum—and screen—for the parking lot. At the southern tip of the site, a partial stone bridge abutment was integrated with new materials to craft an overlook. Finally, a broad allée of littleleaf linden trees (*Tilia cordata*) (rumored to be planted by the city at Dan Kiley's suggestion after the tannery closed in the 1960s) forms a free-floating spine for a portion of the park.

The bulk of "negative" contamination consisted of construction rubble discovered in a gravel pit destined to become the north pond. Excavation of the pond's edge was shifted and the debris capped with clay in situ, creating a subtle hillock at the park's northern tip. Although dumping in derelict lands is a common development practice, it is not an urban legacy the designers chose to focus upon in the park's final design. Constructed in an era when brownfield reclamation was nascent and high-profile competitions for parks were just emerging as popular project types, Mill Race had few precedents to look to for remediative design strategies, but also had little interest in them. Van Valkenburgh notes that in hindsight, the brush with site contamination at Mill Race Park (and, nearly simultaneously, at the Walker Art Center Sculpture Garden extension in Minneapolis) was a "marker of things to come, the beginning of an awareness of dirty stuff on every site." Many of the firm's subsequent projects incorporate more specific design responses to soil and water toxins.

Crisscrossed by defunct dams, covered bridges, and rail lines, the Flatrock River is slow flowing for the most part, and shallow, its waters gliding over gravel bars between eroding sand and gravel banks. Flood stage begins at 9 feet above average levels, at which point 60 percent of the park grounds are submerged; 100-year events are declared when the waters top 16 feet.[4] In conceptualizing the park, one had to take into account that inundation was not a remote possibility but a frequent reality. From the outset, the cyclical processes of regional hydrology were incorporated as a fundamental tool for transforming "vague" terrain into a park landscape.[5] Accordingly, Mill Race Park does not simply observe its hydrologic context, it participates. At the heart of this strategy are the park's core performative systems: the circulation of water, a kind of wet program, and the accommodation of people, the dry program. Mutually these informed the park's topographic tactics, which in turn determined decisions about configuration.

NORTH INDIANAPOLIS ROAD

19

17

18

15

16

8

10

15

1

3

4

5

2

8

12

11

9

6

8

10

7

FLATROCK RIVER

DRIFTWOOD RIVER

EAST FORK WHITE RIVER

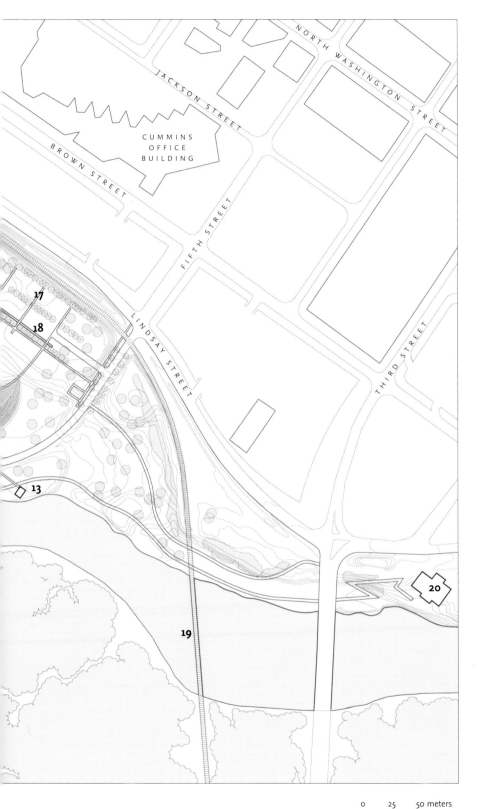

MILL RACE PARK

The downtown core of Columbus is to the upper right; the Flatrock River flows along the site's wooded western boundary. Primary parking is at the remnant walls on the park's east boundary. The loop road and river walk loosely follow the water's edge. The preexisting allée of lindens and MVVA's crescent-shaped amphitheater define the main gathering space. Round Lake is at the park's center. The wetlands lie between the lake and the Flatrock River's edge. MVVA identified the ten sites for the park structures which were subsequently designed by Stanley Saitowitz.

KEY
1 North Lake (preexisting)
2 Round Lake
   with *Metasequoia* Edge
3 Overlook
4 Boathouse
5 Covered Bridge (preexisting)
6 Arbor
7 Fishing Pier
8 Picnic Shelter
9 Basketball Court
10 Bathroom
11 Lake Water Outfall and Sluice
12 Boat Access
13 Tower
14 Amphitheater and Stage
15 Linden Allée (preexisting)
16 Play Area
17 Parking Lots
18 Tannery Wall
19 Louisville and Indiana Railroad
20 Senior Center

CUMMINS OFFICE BUILDING

JACKSON STREET

NORTH WASHINGTON STREET

BROWN STREET

FIFTH STREET

LINDSAY STREET

THIRD STREET

0 25 50 meters

N

0 100 200 feet

Figuration: Topographical Tactics

To begin, two abandoned gravel pits adjacent to the river's edge were reengineered. One became an irregularly shaped pond that transitions between first nature (wilderness: the river) and third nature (art: Round Lake).[6] The second pit, its perimeter transfigured into a perfect circle, became Round Lake. Fourth nature, an industrially driven manipulation of the landscape, is represented by a pair of chutes that conduct the (pumped) outflow of Round Lake back into the river. The sluices subvert nature's paradigm, shortcut riparian patterns, and technologically enhance the water system's operational efficiency. Conceptually, they are an early attempt by Van Valkenburgh to reveal site engineering, an exposure of landscape infrastructure that recalls the contemporaneous, inside-out skin of the Pompidou Center. Collectively the components comprise a chain of water elements that carry pragmatic and symbolic roles within the park's parti (a fusion of purposes that glances sideways to Herbert Bayer's Mill Creek Canyon as a contemporary precedent[7]).
At normal water levels, the river imperceptibly feeds the chain, although the parts appear relatively self-contained. At high water, as determined by their relative elevations, each link along the chain is successively submerged. Because of its height, the lake's round retaining edge and encircling dawn redwoods (*Metasequoia glyptostroboides*, originally planted as flowering cherry trees) are among the last elements to be covered and among the first to reemerge. The Euclidian clarity of the circular lake is a foil for the irregularity of the north pond and the wetland's imprecise degrees of saturation. Closer to the river, the effects of inundation are less managed and last longer.

Spoils from the 450-foot-diameter Round Lake were used to build two elements: a low berm that frames the basketball court, and an immense crescent landform that serves as an amphitheater in the dry season. During floods, the amphitheater appears as an island among treetops. The height and breadth of the crescent provide prospect and create a relationship with the linden allée that suggests boundaries for the park's primary open space. The huge landform measures flood levels, meters sun angles, and brings to mind the earthworks of Native Americans who dwelled in the region. Together Round Lake and the amphitheater compose the heart of the park, thematically and figurally. They engage macro-scaled site cycles and facilitate the alteration of the ground from a field condition when dry to a collection of objects when flooded, enabling several critical positions to be established.

First, as the earliest major built work of an emerging practice, the park is a testament to its time. The circle and crescent can be read as aggressively postmodernist, iconic snippets reassembled as surface inscription. But they go deeper; their deviant formal perfection is the very thing that allows hydrological action to register within the park frame as a civil discourse between culture and nature. The circular lake and crescent amphitheater are not so much about stasis and configuration as about figuring grounds for flux in the landscape. And in this role, they signal a transition in practice and theory toward increased interest in the revelation of site process as civicness, as well as in the poetics of regional materials. Mill Race Park doesn't prioritize

human settlement patterns over environmental forces, but builds upon both
as intertwined systems.

Second, the lake and the landform are essential elements of
orientation within the site structure. They are neutral coordinates: not purely
of the river or the city, they establish a unique locus for the park. With this
simple act of abstraction, raw environment is refined into a perceptible
encounter that exploits the ordinary for the momentary. Perception becomes
program, circumstance becomes content. Since the park cannot be fully known
from a single point in time, circumstances are anticipated but not consistently
predicted. Temporal measures, such as the crest of a flood stage, and the
consequent swing of territorial limits, such as the expanding and receding
wetland floor, calibrate in response to factors far beyond the park's bounds. At
Mill Race Park, geometry is intervention, not structure; via abstraction, isolated
moments call forth meaning from surrounding otherness.

Third, the figures are topographic registrations that question the
truth of the ground plane. The lake is excavated, establishing an alternate
surface of water in place of solid earth. The amphitheater is molded from the
spoils of the lake. Its elevation presents a profile of addition upon the existing
site surface, in counterbalance to the subtractive contour of the lake basin.
This dialectic plays out too in the operative protocols of the two components.
The lake is linked to the wetland and to the larger river system, thus its water
fluctuates in volume and turbidity according to the region's hydro-logic.
On calm days, the smooth lake surface reflects the sky with startling lucidity.
In contrast, the crescent landform is clothed in rooted, opaque turf. The
growth and dormancy phases of the grass are artificially modified through acts
of mowing, aeration, fertilization, and irrigation. The culturated materiality
of the landform's surface, regulated by municipal schedule and budget,
represents control. It is a swelled section of the domesticated suburban plane.
Meanwhile, the lake waters reflect a complex, less managed relationship to

The sluice that feeds water from Round Lake back into the Flatrock River is an instance of visible landscape infrastructure in the park.

nature, particularly as its content is an ever-changing mix of environmental, agricultural, and urban detritus filtered through the intricate wetlands. The lake maintains a minimum depth, but during flood events the water level rises, creating a thickened aqueous section that temporarily detains floodwater before submitting to greater forces and overflowing into surrounding open parklands.

Wet and Dry Program

While the wet program of flood management and water circulation exploits past lands uses—primarily the quarries—to gain form and volume, the dry program of pedestrian and vehicular activities is derived more closely from the overlap of surface patterns of city (the street grid) and river (the oxbow). One set of access pathways and parking extends angular urban orders into the site, leading visitors to specific engagement zones such as the arrival area, the watch tower at the terminus of 5th Street, the concert field, and playgrounds. A second set of circuits includes the sinuous river walk following the site's western edge, a simple network of boardwalks through densely wooded wetlands in the northern tier, and a loop road winding through the site. Along the river walk, riparian growth is managed to open sight lines toward the river and to strengthen the legibility of the groves-and-prairie palette.

Additional dry program moments are distributed throughout the park as micro-destinations that serve specific functions: picnic shelter, restroom, arbor, water pavilion, fishing pier, tower, and viewing deck. At the request of the client, Van Valkenburgh worked with Berkeley-based architect Stanley Saitowitz to site ten structures, each painted red in the fashion of the then recently opened Parc de la Villette. With a wink toward Villette and the eighteenth-century English landscape garden, the elements have been referred to as follies. A different goal, in the landscape architect's mind at least, was to foster William Whyte–style participation in a healthy public sphere of diverse activities and lively spaces. Overall, there is a frugality in the treatment of site materials; affordability and durability became increasingly essential as the design progressed and the construction budget was limited. For example, with regular flooding and ease of maintenance in mind, many of the paved surfaces are reinforced concrete rather than asphalt (which can be peeled up by floods). The steel and glass-block restroom walls are raised to allow flow through; the playground is elevated on a wide earth platform; the amphitheater stage is lodged into the protected higher ground of the crescent landform. Plantings tend to be hardy native species, including grasses that weather drought and native trees that withstand saturated soils.

Conclusions

One of the more remarkable aspects of Mill Race Park is its modesty. There are no acts of ego, despite the grand scale of the amphitheater and the lake. There is little nostalgia, beyond the adaptive reuse of bridges and tannery walls.[8] In fact, as MVVA discovered in decades of subsequent work, subtlety can be of issue when it is confused with loss of critical perspective. When conventionally

The sinuous river walk winds through preexisting groves of native species, tracing a naturalized topography. An irregular, widely spaced row of native sycamore trees occurs at the river side of the path.

negative site conditions such as shifting riverbanks, flooding, contamination, abandoned structures, and incursive native species become points of departure not for acts of erasure but for reconsideration of the real (e)state of the local region, a designer might be accused of timidity. But this is not the case at Mill Race, which points to its importance as a seminal project for a landscape practice as well as for a profession dealing at the time with increasing numbers of marginal sites. Walking through Mill Race is like reading James Joyce. The creative action is not so much about invention as it is about amplification. It is as easy to allow the eye to skim through accounts of insignificant acts and the everyday as to permit the feet to wander along pathways without noting dips in the terrain, variances of light and canopied shadow, the glint of a river bend flowing past a matte gravel bar, waving tips of native grasses. But subconscious responses are what individuate us. To some degree, we are accustomed to being told what to think about a thing by the strength of its identity. It is more difficult, but perhaps more rewarding, to judge a thing alongside others, and its meaning against a moving background of time and circumstance. This situationalism is a strength and a weakness that Mill Race negotiates quietly. By relating to a context greater than the immediate, it reveals forces best understood as part of a continuum. Between permanence and flux, articulate form and unpredictable event, the facts of history and phenomena of materiality, the park asserts a regional relevancy and critical significance.

The growing need for powerful *experiences* that actualize an individual's knowledge of site will drive park making in this generation. In this scenario, participation and permutation produce specificity and viability in the public sphere. Matter matters—nature is not docile but productive and seductive, governed by the potent interaction of environmental and human forces. Public parks occupy this middle landscape that is neither fully technological nor natural, an area of ecological substance plus projective design

View toward picnic lawn from the MVVA-designed amphitheater. The stage and canopy were designed by Stanley Saitowitz.

Below Detail view of the amphitheater, showing the steps within the landform, looking toward the 5th Street connection to downtown.

A series of entry walks pierce the old tannery wall and make evident a remnant industrial fragment in the park.

technique that privileges ambient equations of matter, information, and sensation. Due in part to a fluidity of design intentions over time, Van Valkenburgh's work is a useful cipher for discussing the progression from late modernism through the material vitalism of Big Nature that is emerging in today's progressive landscapes. The major themes expressed at Mill Race—(explicit) form and (cataclysmic) event—gained increasing momentum in the practice of MVVA throughout the 1990s and beyond. Van Valkenburgh's longtime interests in horticulture and landscape phenomena, as well as his design partnership with Laura Solano and Matthew Urbanski, have accumulated into a methodology revolving around a growing interest in exaggerated materiality. Technologically enhanced and environmentally sympathetic, current MVVA projects owe a debt to ideas first realized at Mill Race Park.

View of the new walkway that
cuts through the tannery
wall and connects the parking
lot to the interior of the park.

Notes

1 A graphic formalism in modern landscape architecture was inaugurated in the 1920s–1940s with the Cubist gardens of the Vera brothers, Legrain, Guevrekian, and others. See Dorothée Imbert, *The Modernist Garden in France* (New Haven: Yale University Press, 1993). By the 1940s, formalism in the work of modernists Tunnard, Church, Kiley, Eckbo, and Rose moved fully into three dimensions, using clarity of form to define spatial volumes. See Marc Treib, *Modern Landscape Architecture: A Critical Review* (Cambridge, Massachusetts: MIT Press, 1993). At the end of the 1970s the work of Peter Walker, Martha Schwartz, and others introduced late modernist/minimalist formalism as a fusion of articulated ground plane and spatial volume through the techniques of gesture, seriality, and flatness. See Peter Walker with Cathy Deino Blake, "Minimalist Gardens without Walls," *The Meaning of Gardens*, Mark Francis and Randolph T. Hester, eds. (Cambridge, Massachusetts: MIT Press, 1991).

2 Beginning in the 1940s, galvanized by major funding from the Cummins Engine Foundation and the Irwin Miller family, civic leaders commissioned a string of international designers and artists, resulting in more than fifty notable public buildings, landscapes, and installations. For certain architects and landscape architects, including Eero Saarinen (North Christian Church, 1964) and Dan Kiley (Miller House Garden, 1955, a collaboration with Saarinen and Kevin Roche),

projects in Columbus were instrumental to promoting their careers.

3 The park is downstream but in a portion of the same floodplain as the Miller House Garden, the breakthrough modern masterpiece that used a topographical language and heightened spatial dynamics to communicate a new relationship between the postwar lifestyle and landscape. Similar to the Miller House Garden, although for a public audience rather than a private residence, Mill Race signaled for its era a fresh relationship between society and environment. At the time of the park's inception, renewed interest in the Land Art movement of the 1960s offered a model for "debased sites" as aesthetically valid landscapes (see John Beardsley's discussion of the sympathies between Van Valkenburgh's design philosophy and the works of Robert Smithson in "In the Works," *Design with the Land: Landscape Architecture of Michael Van Valkenburgh*, Brooke Hodge, ed. (New York: Princeton Architectural Press, 1994): 18–27. Entropic and stochastic actions such as inundation, deposition, erosion, growth, and decay began to provide site narrative as well as an ambiguous formalism that differentiated postmodernism in landscape from architecture. Simultaneously, sufficient distance had been gained from the determinism of 1970s-style environmentalism such as Ian McHarg's ecological planning method [see Elizabeth K. Meyer, "The Post-Earth Day Conundrum: Translating Environmental Values into Landscape Design," in *Environmentalism in Landscape Architecture*, Michel Conan,

ed. (Washington, D.C.: Dumbarton Oaks, 2000): 187–244, and Jones & Jones' river planning studies (see Jane Amidon, *Source Books in Landscape Architecture 4: ILARIS, Jones & Jones Puget Sound Plan*, New York: Princeton Architectural Press, 2007)] to permit reengagement with working nature in a critical manner. In contrast, the modernist icon of the Miller House Garden resists its immediate natural and cultural surrounds to a certain degree. It is poised upon an architecturalized earth plinth, raised above the floodplain, its grounds shielded from direct exposure to the suburban milieu by formalized plant materials.

4 This has happened on numerous occasions, repeatedly teaching the settlement of Columbus that it would pay for the convenience of proximity to flowing water with the dangerous inconvenience of flooding. The worst flood on record was in 1913, with a crest of nearly 18 feet. Recent events include two crests in 2006, at 10 and 11 feet, a treacherous 17-foot flood, and a second flood rise at 10 feet in 2005, 14 feet in 2004, 13 feet in 2002, and so on. The 17-foot deluge of 2005 reached the 100-year flood level, and it had significant impacts on the area, rendering major roads impassable, causing evacuations, and wreaking extensive water damage on homes and businesses. Data on the current health and hydrology of the Flatrock and Driftwood river watershed is found on www.in.gov/dnr and www.noaa.gov.

5 In "Terrain Vague," Ignasi de Solà-Morales discusses

"spaces that are internal to the city, but external to its everyday uses." *Anyplace*, Cynthia Davidson, ed. (New York: Anyone Corp/ MIT Press, 1995).

6 See John Dixon Hunt and numerous other garden scholars' writings on first, second, and third natures.

7 Opened in 1982, Bayer's Mill Creek Canyon Earthwork contains stormwater overflow within 2.5 acres of a 100-acre park in Kent, Washington. It was conceived as part of the King County Arts Commission's "Earthworks: Land Reclamation as Sculpture" initiative, which also commissioned an earthwork by Robert Morris in a gravel pit in the same town. See "Work of Art, Work of Earth," by Sheila Farr in the *Seattle Times*, September 7, 2007.

8 Compare this to the isolation and romanticization of industrial remnants in precedents such as Gas Works Park (1975).

Allegheny Riverfront Park

Jane Amidon

Allegheny Riverfront Park
Material, Event, Sensation

ALLEGHENY
RIVERFRONT PARK
Pittsburgh, Pennsylvania
Lower-level park:
3,700 feet long x 31 feet
(average) wide
Upper-level park:
1,920 feet long x 32.5 feet
(average) wide
Completed in 2001

Like most urban centers, the city of Pittsburgh historically arranged its land uses following the logic of topography. Residential development collected at upper elevations, industry (and laborers) located below along the Monongahela and Allegheny riverfronts, with commerce between. For Pittsburgh in particular, throughout the industrial era of the nineteenth and much of the twentieth centuries, the low-lying terrain along the rivers was occupied by toxic activities that produced much of the steel that built modern America. Wealth generated by the refinement and consumption of the region's natural resources allowed steel barons such as Andrew Carnegie to fund cultural foundations and educational institutions and, additionally, to provide grand green spaces for the public. Constructed in the period between 1880 and the 1920s, the well-tended pastoral parks of Pittsburgh perch roughly at an elevation of 1,200 feet and above, neatly corresponding to demographic trends of the time. In the same period, the topographically and socially "negative" lands of ravines and riparian corridors continued to be used for the processing, storage, and transport of undesirable substances and underprivileged populations.[1]

By the 1980s, as the city struggled to redefine its image and economy following the collapse of the steel industry, a reexamination of the relationship between a city and its rivers began. The water's edge was viewed as a potential public amenity in a way that it had not been since the Olmsted brothers' unrealized 1910 proposal for a riverfront park system. In 1994 the Pittsburgh Cultural Trust issued a request for proposals for a half-mile-long linear park between the Sixth and Ninth Avenue bridges. The site consisted of a 1,920-foot-long upper strip lodged between Fort Duquesne Boulevard and a seawall, plus a concrete apron nearly 30 feet below, 3,700 feet long, slivered between the Tenth Street Bypass and the river. The only existing connection between city and river was a pair of infrequently used steel staircases descending from the bridges. Anything brave enough to inhabit the lower level would be swept annually by floods. For the casual observer, there was not enough space to imagine a park of any usefulness. For Carol Brown of the Pittsburgh Cultural Trust, this underutilized, interstitial terrain had the potential to reinvigorate the newly created arts and entertainment district's waterfront edge.

The commission was awarded to Michael Van Valkenburgh Associates, led by principals Michael Van Valkenburgh, Laura Solano, and Matthew Urbanski, with artists Ann Hamilton and Michael Mercil. A long collaborative

The lower-level park's thicket of floodplain trees, nine years after planting.

Expanded axonometric drawing showing the layers of infrastructure that compose the park and create a connection to downtown Pittsburgh.

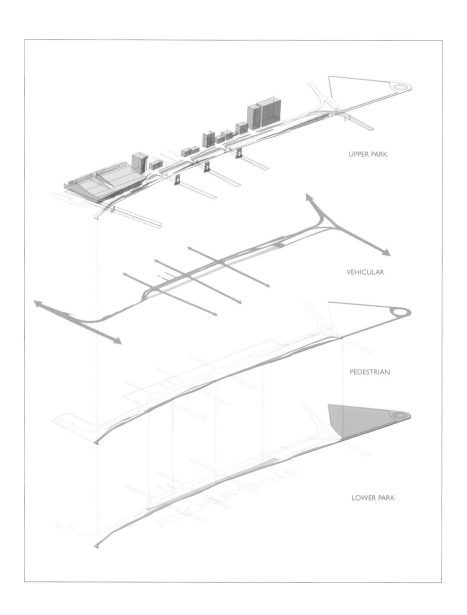

UPPER PARK

VEHICULAR

PEDESTRIAN

LOWER PARK

Left Large-scale detritus deposited by floodwaters on the site before the new park was constructed.

Right The lower park site, about 30 feet wide, was originally an impervious parking lot.

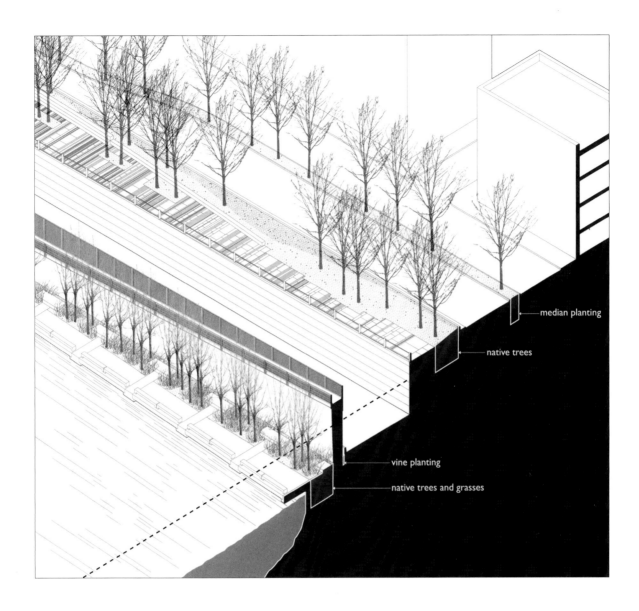

median planting

native trees

vine planting

native trees and grasses

The cross-section shows the relationship between the city (at the upper level), the park (at the upper and lower levels), and the river (lower level).

process was initiated with the goal of creating a park in what one team member described as the "gritty, noisy, impossibly thin reality of the site."[2] From the outset three major challenges were evident: lack of space, severely restricted access, and seasonal flooding. For reasons of creativity, and perhaps sanity, these issues were reimagined to be strange gifts. Site limitations were not new to MVVA; in a collection of earlier projects, site peculiarities led to design innovations that in time became project signatures. For example, the interaction of floodwaters and landforms provided a framework for the design parti at Mill Race Park (Columbus, Indiana, 1993). But here the coincidence of conditions—exacerbated by a tight budget and unexpected discoveries such as a major sewage interceptor and portions of the seawall and lower river-bank backfilled with decades of coal slag—presented an unusually complex

The park was designed to withstand the force of regular flood events from the Allegheny River.

Below Silt and flood debris deposited on the ramp by the flood of September 2004.

environment from which to craft a park.[3] In addition, overlapping jurisdictions made for lengthy negotiations. Traffic lanes were governed by state and federal highway commissions, the sidewalk and seawall by the city, the intersecting bridges by the county. The river water itself was under federal authority, and a matrix of public and private utilities ran beneath the site. Much of the designers' early efforts revolved not around gaining approval from the client for the master plan but around solidifying consensus among competing interests about *why* to implement strategic moves. Although it was clear that funding was not in place for the entire project, the design team negotiated its contract to include both upper and lower parks through design development. This tactic allowed the composite park to be discussed as an intrinsically unified effort, and likely generated greater support for completing the project in its entirety rather than stopping after implementation of the first half.

Finding Space for a Park

On the upper level, Fort Duquesne Boulevard offered both promise and problems. Six lanes of traffic, a median, and a 6-foot-wide sidewalk running parallel to the seawall featured broad views of the flowing Allegheny, the Three Sisters bridges, and the revived architectural face of the cultural district. Although the design team readily came up with the idea to subtract the median from the boulevard and add it to the sidewalk, it took weeks of scrutinizing urban highway codes to find standards that would fit the designers' intentions to shift the strip west, doubling the width of the upper park to an average of 32 feet. While this is a relatively small act, its symbolism as a seed for future green networks should be noted. Many U.S. cities are faced today with the consequences of having given over waterfronts to automobiles in the postwar era of highway infrastructure projects. Only a few, such as Portland, Oregon's Eastbank Esplanade,[4] are finding means to incrementally thread open-space networks within and alongside aging infrastructure, avoiding the exorbitant financial and ecological expense of reworking the urban landscape on the massive scale of Boston's Big Dig.

On the lower level, almost 30 feet beneath the urban plane, on constructed terrain not figured in the city's plan, one looks upward into the city's underside to see its armatures and abutments and instruments. Here direct proximity to the flowing river presents a (sub)liminal spectacle that plays night and day, all year, preceding the city as a regional artery and whose true allegiance is to a distant fact of geography, the Gulf of Mexico. But at this exact point, thousands of cubic square feet per second of the region's water coalesce from the upper reaches of Pennsylvania's Allegheny Plateau and the Southern Tier of New York state, having made its way through branches of the watershed, on the verge of marrying with the Monongahela to form the Ohio River.[5] Anything placed here is subject to severe flood of up to 20 feet, brutal ice-floe barrages, and, sometimes, loose and very large flotsam such as pleasure boats and barges that have lost their moorings. Like the upper park, originally there wasn't enough width alongside the river to fit a public space of any consequence. The solution became a cantilevered walkway that increases the usable width of the existing concrete apron from less than 15 feet to an average of 31 feet. The Army Corps of Engineers restricted the design team and its engineer, Arup, to four piers in the riverbed. These are located at the walk's widest stretch beneath the Seventh Street bridge and help support a system of inverted T-beams with precast concrete panels. The cantilever's counterweights pose a technological counterpoint to the messy nature of the lower park: their measured, serial placement and angular smoothness contrast with a loose tumble of rough boulders, unpredictable density of plantings, and fluctuating waters that bracket the walkway.

　　With park space wrought from river and highway, the dramatic vertical separation of the two levels remained an issue. The answer became an equation of utility and experience: two massive ramps at first envisioned as open steelwork reminiscent of the nearby bridges, but later realized as seemingly solid concrete wedges. Descending 25 feet from the Sixth and Ninth Street bridges over a length of 350 feet, the paired ramps inhabit the seam of river and city. Their bases are tapered, creating a smaller footprint for more planting room on the lower park and a more generous width at the upper access points. While aspects of the upper and lower parks operate at the intimate scale of the individual user, the ramps speak directly to the city. In the tradition of grand public works, the ramps are symmetrical, and nearly neutral in their aesthetics and orientation—like the bridges that run perpendicular to the water's flow to link gridirons at the urban shore, there is no challenge to

the rules of efficiency that govern infrastructure. The ramps play a service role, proffering a stage so frank in formal simplicity that it is nearly invisible at the same moment that it is the biggest, boldest thing around. Within urban landscapes, beauty often is sought in the intricate and unexpected, but in this case it is found in a kind of slowness, a conscious pragmatism.

Scissoring

Organized as a tripartite linear progression—an upper and a lower plane connected by a diagonal—Allegheny Riverfront Park is unlike conventional spatial models of the pastoral city park or a formal civic space. Its pieces provide a template of movement more closely aligned with precedents of quays and parkways, two typologies born from the cohabitation of urban and natural systems. The scissoring gesture of the ramps unfolds and elongates the passage from one level to the other, emphasizing the dialectic between upper and lower environments and engaging at a small scale the physiography of Pittsburgh as the city ascends from riverbed and floodplain up densely settled hillsides. To a significant extent, circulation equals configuration, promoting movement as program. The attenuation of experience, the duration of perception, is a tool used to elevate the subjective intake of temporal and spatial orientation.

The utility of this formal arrangement stems from the immediate conditions of urban topography, but its impact emerges from regional allegories. Most simply, each part of the park refers paradigmatically to something greater than itself. In its spatial arrangement and use of bluestone with familiar street trees, the upper level is a synecdoche of civilized, civic terrain. In a similar manner, the lower level is modeled upon the wildness of the river and the received textures and cycles of the riparian corridor. The concrete ramps speak at the monumental, infrastructural volume of Pittsburgh's highway decks, tunnels, and bridges. There is a montage-like quality to the pieces and their textures from a distance; the upper, lower, and ramp elements compress to read against one another, again making reference to context, but this time at the comprehensive scale of Pittsburgh piled upon its steep topography.

Hypercontext

At Allegheny Riverfront Park, the arrangement and amplification of topographic, geologic, and vegetative states is extremely specific and persistent. An exaggerated contextualization is found at the scale of site detail, where common materials are exploited for their most literal qualities. The variations of grain, grit, density, porosity, moisture response, light reactivity, color mutation, growth habit, and other peculiarities of paving and planting types enable experiential sensations—micro events of a sort—that are deeply of the region but specific to this place, this time.

On the upper level the park opens at each street corner in a small plaza. A modulated rhythm of bluestone paving strips begins here, then shifts size, tone, and cleft as it spreads inward. The surface pattern compresses from

NINTH STREET

SEVENTH STREET

FORT DUQUESNE BOULEVARD

6

3   2   3
      4
          1

TENTH STREET   BYPASS

7   7
10   9   9   9
          8   8

NINTH STREET BRIDGE

SEVENTH STREET BRIDGE

A   L   L   E   G   H   E   N

ALLEGHENY RIVERFRONT PARK

Downtown Pittsburgh is at the
top of the drawing. Point State
Park, the convergence of the
Allegheny and the Monongahela
rivers that forms the beginning
of the Ohio River, is downstream
to the right.

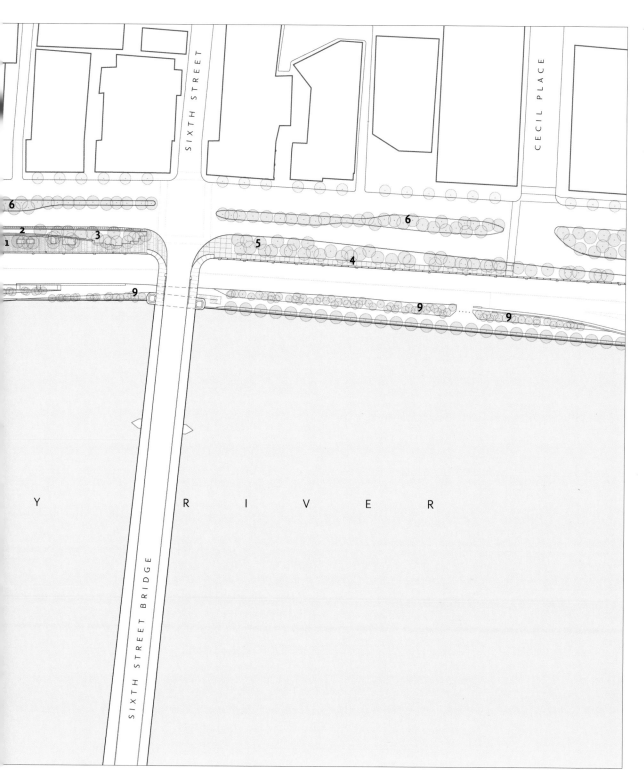

SIXTH STREET

CECIL PLACE

6

2   3

1

9

5

4

6

9

9

Y   R   I   V   E   R

SIXTH STREET BRIDGE

UPPER LEVEL PARK

1 Bluestone Pavement
2 300 ft Bluestone Bench
3 Plant Bed
4 Overlook
5 Treed Lawn
6 Planted Median

LOWER LEVEL PARK

7 350 ft Accessible Ramp
8 Cantilevered Walkway
9 Plant Bed with Floodplain Species
10 Overlook Platform

0   25   50 meters

0   100   200 feet

N

6-foot-square paving stones at the entry plazas into 4- and then 2-inch-wide slivers that vary in length from 18 to 36 inches. The bluestone, a metamorphic sandstone found throughout Pennsylvania and upstate New York, was difficult to spec because of the thinness of its cut and the fact that the design team originally hoped to lay the strips on their side, exposing the bedding plane of sedimentary layers. Rather than draw the entire paving pattern and insist on exact execution, the designers gave the contractors a set of parameters: across the east-west width, set ten rows of 2-inch pieces, then six row of the next, four rows of the next, and so on. For each 2-inch-wide paver, the length could be 18 to 36 inches. No joints can line up, all pieces have to be rectangular, the colors must vary. The subcontractors were liberated to make decisions within those rules—a process that the design team feels allowed a sense of craft to emerge, which despite the low-bid status of the project, elevated the final results.

In section the surface dips 30 inches as the park widens at its center points between bridges; earth stacked behind massive, natural cleft bluestone blocks increases the sense of separation from the traffic of Fort Duquesne Boulevard. A monoculture of London plane trees set in the earthen berm (with mixed cultivars to maintain genetic diversity) reinforces the embrace of the cupped land; others emerge directly from the pavement and filter the view without explicitly framing it. As one looks outward from these expanded moments, the dipped surface rises subtly to meet the grade of the existing handrail at the seawall, creating an artificial horizon. In tandem with the plan's expanding and contracting bluestone surface, the sectional play effects a dynamic quality. The quiet concavity is a result of the designers' decision to keep rather than mask a preexisting sink in the profile of the seawall. In the end, that simple choice saved much money and reenforced the perception of subspaces within the upper park's progression.

On the lower level, dense massings of species cataloged by the designers on trips upriver suggest a native but intensified material palette. River birch, silver maple, poplar, and mixed grasses were selected for their field-grown, noncultivated habit. Less expensive to install and genetically programmed to recover after flood events, the floodplain species present a heightened material state of vegetation that is authored, but to a large degree feral. One wonders if it is possible to present such ecological associations and material behaviors as noncultural acts; the very definition of what most conceive of as "nature" is derived intrinsically from our ideas of self and societal values.[6] Within the tumult of riverside plantings, a crust of boulders stands out against the smooth ramp backdrop. The weight of the boulders secures the trees' root-balls and helps prevent soil scouring when floodwaters pour across the lower park. They appear as found objects in some geologic sculpture garden, offering a regionally derived lithic alternative to the universality of poured concrete surfaces. The selection of raw bluestone boulders on the lower level corresponds to the use of processed bluestone pavers in the upper park, encouraging an awareness of the untamed and the refined versions of our relationship to natural materials.

Paralleling the base of the ramp, the lower walkway is imprinted with native reeds that seem to flow in the direction of the river waters. Ironically this gesture of localness could not have been more contrived: protected by law, the reeds couldn't be harvested upriver, where artist Ann Hamilton first saw them. So the team sent seeds to be grown in Florida; the harvested grasses were express mailed back to Pittsburgh and kept in mesh bags suspended in the Allegheny River until ready for pressing into the walkway. Over time the reeds washed out, leaving imprints that evoke fronds and the scars of overly enthusiastic snow removal. When the walk swings out around the Seventh Street bridge abutment it reorients the viewer away from the city and toward the river's breadth, and pushes down toward the water—another subtle but essential sectional play, as with the sitting areas of the upper park. At this point the surface becomes blank, signaling that the body is no longer rooted to solid ground as the river incurs depth. Like the bluestone rhythm of the upper walkway, information about place is taken in simultaneously by eye and foot.

On the outer surface, facing the river, the battered base of the ramps is stained in warm tones that anticipate eventual water marks and engage the mutable colors of stone and plant materials. On the ramps' inner edge, rising above the Tenth Street Bypass, a chain-link vine scrim supports growing curtains of Virginia creeper. Appearing from various angles to be highway sign, security fence, or part industrial trellis, once covered with greenery the scrim is a living vertical plane equal to the inert infrastructural status of the ramps. The ramps themselves reveal calculations of minute variances: by closely examining ADA codes, the design team found an opportunity to calibrate the ramp sections, landings, and rails with a continuous inclined curb that avoids a slope-landing-slope-landing profile and creates a pure wedge form. This is intended to be the "desirable experience" of access—meaning that if users comply, there is a role reversal in which the Sixth and Ninth Street stairways are secondary to the ramps as the primary circulation route.

An undulating bronze rail provides unexpected inflection to the ramps' monolithic character. Sculpted over months of modeling in Mercil and Hamilton's studio, the rail creates a balcony-like effect along the descent. Among other direct references, the artists looked at a painting by Georgia O'Keeffe depicting a line moving up and back into a sheet of paper, and at Carl Andre's broken line snaking across a meadow, to get at the idea of horizontal movement and twisting motion. Never able to draw the effect, the team carved foam and cast eleven sets of four pieces, each 16 feet long, which on site were randomly selected and rotated counterclockwise or end-to-end to ensure a ribbonlike form. The rail has a sense of selfness, and nondeliberateness that is close to animation. The eye sees this, the hand feels it, the ear hears the passing cars a thin scrim away (and some distance below), all nested within the roll of the river. The ramps themselves become their own sort of landscape, integrative but disconnected from the upper and lower realms.

Native reeds were pressed
into the surface of the concrete
paving on the lower level
to recall the native river edge
ecology.

The indigenous Pennsylvania
bluestone paving on the upper
level uses the material language
found in other locations in
Pittsburgh.

The vine scrim on the highway side of the adjacent four-lane highway. The vine is Virginia creeper, a species highly tolerant of urban pollutants.

Right The Ann Hamilton bronze rail reaches like a tree branch.

Opposite To conserve budget, existing concrete was complemented with indestructible concrete benches and thickets of seedless cottonwood trees.

Tangible Inhabitant

In recent years the practice of Michael Van Valkenburgh Associates has segued through distinct phases, moving from a late modernist stance to a current interest in regional materiality. Essential to this conceptual transformation is the articulation of site matter, not as a diagram or index but as an elucidation of environmental logic that encompasses cultural and ecological will. In many ways, the interaction of matter and climate (the meta code) at Allegheny Riverfront Park was an early hallmark of this larger project. The combined upper and lower parks exaggerate their tectonics and vegetal presence to supersede programmatic definition, deriving identity from expressed circulation, transformation of the local, and seasonal variation. There is an intention that visitors are aggressively enveloped within a sequence of passive constructs: individual action—movement and perception—is required to engage the linear park and to comprehend the clever conciliation of our notions of the civic versus the natural. There's no real choice about how to move through the linear waterfront. Like driving through the city or floating down the river, you have to do it to get it. There is no overarching perspective, no one photograph to capture. This is a park that chooses to heighten the willfulness of its surroundings instead of promoting itself as a destination distinct from context. It's very much about a piece of Pittsburgh, both lowbrow and highbrow, and about the public's ability (or lack thereof) to see the city and the river for merely what they are: a collective expression of diverse forces.

Completed after nearly a decade of research, design, financing, and construction (the lower park opened in 1998, the upper in 2001), the two linear strips and conjoining ramps that constitute Allegheny Riverfront Park offer a significant example of a highly constrained site made over into a desirable urban space. The design team discarded conventional parameters of park making, allowing invention to emerge in several ways: first, in wringing habitable space from highway and river; then, by scissoring monumental circulation elements to build an experience of movement and duration, lightness and gravity; and finally, by customizing installation methods to coax contextual information, affordability, and resilience from urban, geologic, hydrologic, and horticultural materials. In the end the primary challenges of the original site—lack of space, severely restricted accessibility, and flooding—do not compromise the park, perhaps offering proof that material and event now provide content. Urban parks such as this are not scenic but are dynamic, intrinsic inhabitants of their complex, fluxing environments. Parks such as this are not a diversion, not a reorientation from difficult contexts to a hypothetical place. Here the park and its tangible behaviors are fodder for real city life.

Notes

1 This information was gathered by Jacob Boswell in a graduate studio, *Continuous, Productive Urban Landscapes,* conducted at the Knowlton School of Architecture in 2006.

2 See *Source Books in Landscape Architecture 1: MVVA's Allegheny Riverfront Park,* Jane Amidon, ed. (New York: Princeton Architectural Press, 2005) for comments from each member of the design team.

3 Contemporaneous projects in the United States with similar site challenges include Seattle's Olympic Sculpture Park, which solved comparable access and elevation issues with a massive cap that functions as a new ground plane, and New York's Hudson River Park, which employs various reclamation methods for incorporating urban and defunct industrial infrastructures.

4 Designed by the landscape architecture firm Mayer/ Reed and opened in 2001 after four years of construction, the Vera Katz Eastbank Esplanade negotiates significant transportation and industrial armatures. The project provides a 1.5-mile pedestrian walk and bike-way on the banks of the Willamette River, and includes a 1,200-foot-long floating promenade as a partial solution to incorporating public space within urban infrastructure. See the 2004 ASLA Professional Awards for images and information (*www.asla.org*).

5 See *www.noaa.gov* for information on flow rates and water levels on the Allegheny, Monongahela, and Ohio rivers, and pertinent articles about Ohio River watershed flood events and civil engineering efforts gathered by the U.S. Corps of Engineers on *www.usace.army.mil/publications.*

6 See discussions by Neil Evernden and Eugene Hargrove about identity, artifice, art, and nature, in particular: "essence precedes existence" versus "existence precedes essence." In *Environmental Ethics: Divergence and Convergence,* Susan J. Armstrong and Richard G. Botzler, eds. (New York: McGraw-Hill, 1993).

Herman Miller Factory

Elissa Rosenberg

Herman Miller Factory
Suburban Sublime

HERMAN MILLER
FACTORY
Canton, Georgia
70 acres
Completed in 2001

It is rare that landscape operates as both a functioning system and a powerful formal idea. Herman Miller Cherokee, a factory designed by MVVA with architects Scogin Elam and Bray, introduces a new ecological functionality to the suburban industrial landscape. Set on a 70-acre site in a rapidly suburbanizing rural area in Cherokee County, Georgia, some 35 miles north of Atlanta, the project succeeds at integrating landscape with architecture, and engineering with elegant economy. The designers have transformed a potentially sprawling, anonymous building and landscape into a starkly beautiful place.

In most landscape architectural projects, the network of support systems that enables a landscape to function is buried, masked, or made merely incidental to the design. At Herman Miller Cherokee, in contrast, the site infrastructure provides the framework for an evocative formal language, recovering a sense of the "comprehensiveness" that characterized the early years of the landscape architecture profession, when design and engineering were inseparable.[1] The technical and ecological challenges of the site inspired a spirit of formal invention, creating an expressive working landscape using simple materials and techniques.

In the mid-1990s, Herman Miller, Inc., decided to consolidate three Georgia factories on a single site east of Canton, Georgia, a growing area for manufacturing and agribusiness.[2] They selected the Atlanta-based architecture firm Scogin Elam and Bray, which had designed several Herman Miller factories since the 1970s, in both Georgia and Michigan.[3] The architects brought MVVA, their long-standing collaborators, onto the design team, joining Eberly & Associates Inc., a civil engineering firm based in Atlanta. The Cherokee plant was planned for the fabrication, assembly, and distribution of office systems, and the production process set up a clear design logic from the start. This was a low-budget project with a big program on a relatively small site, with no budget allocated initially for landscape. The program included 330,000 square feet of free-span manufacturing space planned for twenty-four-hour operation, as well as expansive areas of surface parking for inventory management and storage, requiring 120 semi-trailers, and employee parking for 550 cars. The site was an old pasture on a steep knoll, bounded by floodplain on three sides, and a state highway on the fourth. It was selected in part for its location near the intersection of major interstate and state highways. Easy access to transportation was a significant factor that far outweighed the physical limitations of the terrain.[4]

The parking lot becomes a hybrid landscape—a paved plane alternating with constructed wetlands that collect and filter runoff. Vertical elements provide spatial structure: hedgerows composed of a random mix of lowland species edge the wetlands, and overscaled wooden telephone poles transform a mundane parking lot into a ceremonial space of arrival.

Sketch showing the relationships among functions:
shipping, receiving, fabrication
and assembly, parking.

Site Organization

As on most industrial sites, the plan of Herman Miller Cherokee is organized
to maximize the efficiency of vehicular access. The site functions as an
extension of the global transportation networks that sustain production; thus
the expansive interior space required for fabrication and assembly is matched
by even more expansive areas of service flowing into and out of the site,
providing for the delivery of raw materials and the distribution of goods.
Fabrication and assembly occur in two connecting sheds, flanked by a large
receiving area on one side and shipping on the other.

The plan maintains the inevitable relationship to the road that
has come to define industrial and suburban planning. However, to restore the
experience of entry that has disappeared in the service-dominated industrial
plan, the entry sequence has been inverted. Shipping and receiving areas
are kept in the front portion of the site and the front door is brought to the

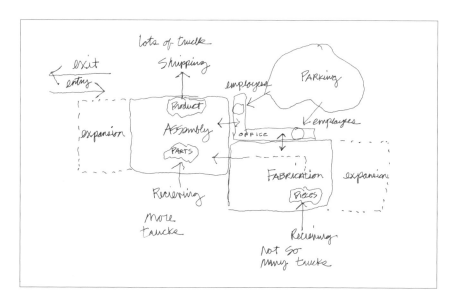

back, along with the requisite adjacent employee parking. By distinguishing
front from back, two distinct arrival sequences are created; the everyday
routine of the factory worker is acknowledged and separated from the
production cycle of truck transport. This strategy allows for a different program, scale, and architectural treatment of the back of the site. A thin,
transparent L-shaped bar of offices wraps the back of the two staggered sheds,
opening up the factory to the southeast and orienting it toward panoramic
views of the Etowah River and the hills beyond.

Hydrology and Ground

The shaping of the ground is the starting point of the landscape design
at Herman Miller Cherokee. According to project landscape architect Matthew
Urbanski, the topographical strategy developed from two basic decisions.
The first was to transform the enormous amount of earthwork required to fit

The extent of regrading necessary to expose the bedrock
in the front retention basin is
visible in this aerial view of
the site during construction.
Above the excavated area is the
semi-trailer parking area, a
courtyard defined by oversized
tilt-up concrete walls.

An early concept sketch by
Matthew Urbanski, exploring
the potential of the Z-shaped
layout of parking and wetlands.

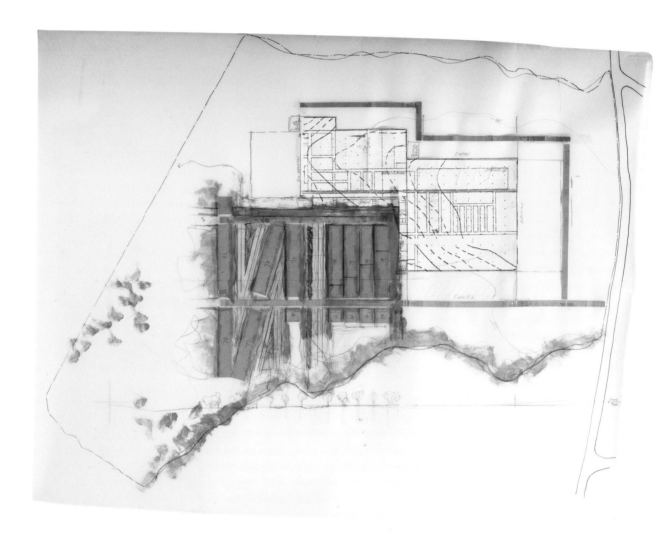

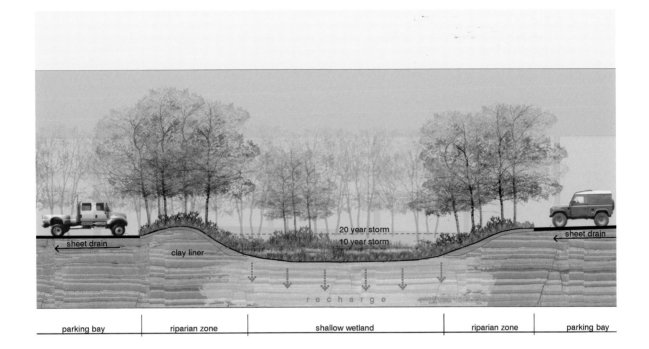

sheet drain

clay liner

20 year storm
10 year storm

sheet drain

r e c h a r g e

| parking bay | riparian zone | shallow wetland | riparian zone | parking bay |

The section through the parking lot illustrates the simplicity of the system: water sheeting across the pavement is collected and filtered within the wetland trays, then percolates back into the soil.

the program on the rolling topography into an opportunity for place making. The second decision was to prevent the degradation of the Etowah River and its tributaries, which border the site, by filtering and storing the large volumes of storm runoff that would be generated by acres of new impervious surfaces. The on-site treatment of stormwater became an organizing idea that shaped the overall plan and section of the site. However, instead of resorting to the ubiquitous detention pond found on most large-scale suburban developments, the landscape architects incorporated some of the stormwater detention into the parking lot itself, by creating a hybrid ground composed of interlocking areas of pavement and wetlands. Curbs and drains are eliminated in the back of the site, and the earth is graded at a consistent 5 percent slope to direct runoff away from the building and drain the parking lot. An early sketch reveals the initial exploration of the parking lot as a sliced plane of alternating solid and porous ground. Although the number of parking spaces was reduced in the final scheme, the parking lot maintains the angled Z-shaped geometry of this first diagram, pulling apart the bays to follow the existing topography and allowing them to drain to a series of wedge-shaped wetlands embedded within the asphalt. The compositional effect of the wetlands' crisp triangular geometry is exaggerated by the uniformly engineered 3:1 banks defining their edges. Together they highlight the abstract, constructed quality of the wetlands that are carved out of the pavement to create a hybrid ground. The Z shape brings the two functions together in one space, interlocked as a single formal idea.

The wetlands are designed to collect and filter the runoff from the parking lot—an area of almost 5 acres—as well as cleanse the building gray water. Adjustable weirs control the water levels, and the terraced configuration

HERMAN MILLER
FACTORY

Site plan showing the
location of the factory on top
of the knoll, fronting the
state highway and bounded
by floodplain on three sides.

KEY

1 Fabrication
2 Assembly
3 Receiving
4 Future Expansion
5 Shipping
6 Offices
7 Tree-lined Entry Drive
8 Parking
9 Stormwater Terrace
10 Overflow
11 Creek
12 Retention Pond
13 Meadow with Exposed Bedrock

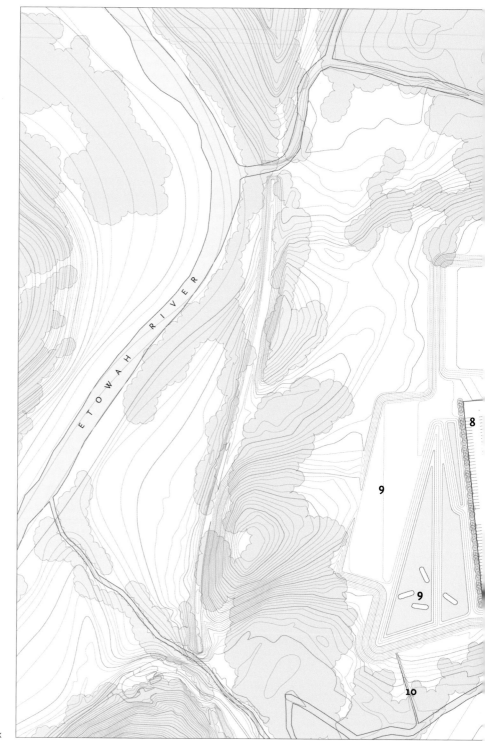

3

12

1

4

2

4

13

6

12

8

9

9

5

7

9

11

B A L L   G R O U N D   H I G H W A Y

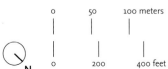

0   50   100 meters

N   0   200   400 feet

Hydrological diagram of the site indicating the flow of runoff from the roof and paved areas and the capacities of the wetlands.

Below The highest wetland terrace receives runoff from three bays of parking. A mixed deciduous hedgerow, planted originally with liner stock, establishes the division between parking and wetland terrace.

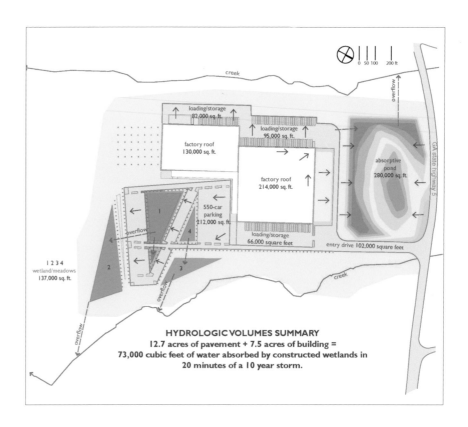

creek

0 50 100   200 ft

loading/storage
82,000 sq. ft.

loading/storage
95,000 sq. ft.

factory roof
130,000 sq. ft.

factory roof
214,000 sq. ft.

absorptive
pond
280,000 sq. ft.

CA state highway 5

overflow

550-car
parking
212,000 sq. ft.

overflow

1 2 3 4
wetland/meadows
137,000 sq. ft.

loading/storage
66,000 square feet

entry drive 102,000 square feet

creek

overflow

overflow

HYDROLOGIC VOLUMES SUMMARY
12.7 acres of pavement + 7.5 acres of building =
73,000 cubic feet of water absorbed by constructed wetlands in
20 minutes of a 10 year storm.

A retention pond at the front of the site collects runoff from the roof and the truck loading area. The pond is bounded on one side by a layered planting of river birch and on the other by exposed bedrock and native prairie.

allows the embedded trays to flow downslope in series, creating two integrated networks. Each network flows to an overflow inlet designed to drain excess volumes of water directly to the surrounding creeks during larger storms. The stormwater that flows off of the 8 acres of rooftop and almost 8 acres of impervious surface in the loading and storage area is treated in a separate subsurface system, collected in a large retention pond at the front of the site. Like the parking wetlands, the retention pond was designed to fill in with marsh vegetation. The pond is ringed with a row of river birch, and today its interior has mostly filled in with successional vegetation. The wetlands and pond have succeeded in creating new habitat, although their effectiveness at pollutant uptake has not yet been monitored.

The project has been written about primarily as an early exemplar of a surface stormwater system using constructed wetlands.[5] But it is more than an innovative drainage solution, a means of "managing" water. It is a project that builds a formal language directly from the act of building the site. The ground of the parking area is sculpted into an expansive tilted plane to allow water to sheet over its surface. This effect is further enhanced by eliminating curbs (rather than provide curb openings, as is more typically seen in surface systems), exaggerating the plane of pavement by stripping away the conventional details associated with it. The ground plane is abstracted and minimally articulated, with the exception of the rich texture and color of the marsh vegetation—a mix of sedges, cattails, and iris.

The ground appears engineered throughout; it is planar and abstract, emphasizing the way the new topography was made. Around the building the precisely angled berm maintains the clarity of the plinth that was leveled to build the vast structure on what was once a rounded knoll. The plinth's even slopes form a threshold to the building, marking the entrance with a casually monumental stair and ramp incised within the berm. The sculptural quality of the berm is accentuated by the added surface texture of ground-cover; a pure stand of little bluestem (*Schizachyrium scoparium*), a local native grass, was specified to create an extensive and uniform mass on the slope.[6]

Function and Ritual

What is most powerful about the project is the way it seems to operate at two registers: the outsized scale of production and the daily texture of experience. The site design reflects a careful negotiation between these two realms. The systemic scale is evoked by heightening and celebrating the sense of expan-siveness. "We chose not to domesticate," says Merrill Elam.[7] Both the architecture and landscape defer to the scale of production and find grandeur in its dimensions, seeking what Matthew Urbanski has called a "suburban sublime." There is no fussy detail. Instead, architecture and landscape are kept abstract and broadly gestural. However, this is not an "industrial sublime," bringing to mind images of nineteenth-century machinery, mines, or blast furnaces, but rather the sublime of the wide open spaces and endless highways that support American industry and suburbia alike.[8]

MVVA addresses the realm of individual experience not by scaling down to create a sense of "human scale" as palliative for the overscaled dimensions of production, but precisely by exploiting extent, openness, and monumentality as qualities that will dramatize the daily routines of workers, bringing a sense of ritual to otherwise mundane, functional spaces. The entrance to the site provides one of its key sublime moments. With the front door moved to the rear, employee arrival is drawn out into a long processional sequence. The entry drive to the parking lot is designed as an extended axial allée, defined by an immense 30-foot wall of concrete tilt-up panels on one side and a row of tulip poplars (*Liriodendron tulipifera*) on the other, framing a view of the distant hills. The truck loading dock at the entrance also provides the occasion for an extravagant gesture. The concrete panel wall that forms the allée serves to enclose the loading dock and storage area, transforming it into an honorific courtyard space. The simple symmetry of the walls and their exaggerated height give the loading court the appearance of a surreal "court of honor," animated by the movement of semi-trailers. In each case, the functional spaces of the site are given architectural presence, acknowledging the human dimension of production.

The use of overscaled elements is perhaps most enigmatic in the employee parking lot. Irregular rows of 30-foot-high, rustic wooden telephone poles rise out of the flat plane of pavement to provide night lighting. They are rhythmically aligned in the parking bays; some of the poles are empty, and some are fitted with simple floodlights, pooling the cars with light. The